Of God and Men

by A. W. TOZER

§

CHRISTIAN PUBLICATIONS, INC.
HARRISBURG, PENNSYLVANIA

Christian Publications, Inc.
25 S. 10th Street, P.O. Box 3404
Harrisburg, PA 17105

The mark of ☯ *vibrant faith*

ISBN 0-87509-254-3

Contents

3

Foreword

THE TITLE of this book gives sufficient indication of what the reader will find in it.

God and men and their relation to each other—this I believe to be all that really matters in this world, and that is what I have written about here.

As a confirmed believer in the Man Christ Jesus as Redeemer and Lord my thoughts naturally arrange themselves around Christ, His teachings, His claims and His church.

To my fellow pilgrims on the way to Zion I offer this book for whatever good they may be able to extract from it. And to our Lord be the praise always.

A. W. TOZER.

Toronto, Ont., Canada

The Report of the Watcher

WERE SOME watcher or holy one from the bright world above to come among us for a time with the power to diagnose the spiritual ills of church people there is one entry which I am quite sure would appear on the vast majority of his reports: *Definite evidence of chronic spiritual lassitude; level of moral enthusiasm extremely low.*

What makes this condition especially significant is that Americans are not naturally an unenthusiastic people. Indeed they have a world-wide reputation for being just the opposite. Visitors to our shores from other countries never cease to marvel at the vigor and energy with which we attack our problems. We live at a fever pitch, and whether we are erecting buildings, laying highways, promoting athletic events, celebrating special days or welcoming returning heroes we always do it with an exaggerated flourish. Our building will be taller, our highway broader, our athletic contest more colorful, our celebration more elaborate and more expensive than would be true anywhere else on earth. We walk faster, drive faster, earn more, spend more and run a higher blood pressure than any other people in the world.

In only one field of human interest are we slow and apathetic: that is the field of personal religion. There for some strange reason our enthusiasm lags. Church people habitually approach the matter of their personal relation to God in a dull, half-hearted way which is altogether out of keeping with their general temperament and wholly inconsistent with the importance of the subject.

It is true that there is a lot of religious activity among us. Interchurch basketball tournaments, religious splash parties followed by devotions, weekend camping trips with a Bible quiz around the fire, Sunday school picnics, building fund drives and ministerial breakfasts are with us in unbelievable numbers, and they are carried on with typical American gusto. It is when we enter the sacred precincts of the heart's personal religion that we suddenly lose all enthusiasm.

So we find this strange and contradictory situation: a world of noisy, headlong religious activity carried on without moral energy or spiritual fervor. In a year's travel among the churches one scarcely finds a believer whose blood count is normal and whose temperature is up to standard. The flush and excitement of the soul in love must be sought in the New Testament or in the biographies of the saints; we look for them in vain among the professed followers of Christ in our day.

Now if there is any reality within the whole sphere

of human experience that is by its very nature worthy to challenge the mind, charm the heart and bring the total life to a burning focus, it is the reality that revolves around the Person of Christ. If He is who and what the Christian message declares Him to be, then the thought of Him should be the most exciting, the most stimulating, to enter the human mind. It is not hard to understand how Paul could join wine and the Spirit in one verse: "Be not drunk with wine, wherein is excess; but be filled with the Spirit" (Eph. 5: 18). When the Spirit presents Christ to our inner vision it has an exhilarating effect on the soul much as wine has on the body. The Spirit-filled man may literally dwell in a state of spiritual fervor amounting to a mild and pure inebriation.

God dwells in a state of perpetual enthusiasm. He is delighted with all that is good and lovingly concerned about all that is wrong. He pursues His labors always in a fullness of holy zeal. No wonder the Spirit came at Pentecost as the sound of a rushing mighty wind and sat in tongues of fire on every forehead. In so doing He was acting as one of the Persons of the blessed Godhead.

Whatever else happened at Pentecost, one thing that cannot be missed by the most casual observer was the sudden upsurging of moral enthusiasm. Those first disciples burned with a steady, inward fire. They were enthusiastic to the point of complete abandon.

Dante, on his imaginary journey through hell,

came upon a group of lost souls who sighed and moaned continually as they whirled about aimlessly in the dusky air. Virgil, his guide, explained that these were the "wretched people," the "nearly soulless," who while they lived on earth had not moral energy enough to be either good or evil. They had earned neither praise nor blame. And with them and sharing in their punishment were those angels who would take sides neither with God nor Satan. The doom of all of the weak and irresolute crew was to be suspended forever between a hell that despised them and a heaven that would not receive their defiled presence. Not even their names were to be mentioned again in heaven or earth or hell. "Look," said the guide, "and pass on."

Was Dante saying in his own way what our Lord had said long before to the church of Laodicea: "I would thou wert cold or hot. So then because thou art lukewarm, and neither cold nor hot, I will spue thee out of my mouth"?

The low level of moral enthusiasm among us may have a significance far deeper than we are willing to believe.

We Must Have Better Christians

To TALK OF "better" Christians is to use language foreign to many persons. To them all Christians are alike; all have been justified and forgiven and are the children of God, so to make comparisons between them is to suggest division and bigotry and any number of horrible things.

What is forgotten is that a Christian is a born-one, an embodiment of growing life, and as such may be retarded, stunted, undernourished or injured very much as any other organism. Favorable conditions will produce a stronger and healthier organism than will adverse conditions. Lack of proper instructions, for instance, will stunt Christian growth. A clear example of this is found in Acts 19, where an imperfect body of truth had produced a correspondingly imperfect type of Christian. It took Paul, with a fuller degree of truth, to bring these stunted disciples into a better and healthier spiritual state.

Unfortunately it is possible for a whole generation of Christians to be victims of poor teaching, low moral standards and unscriptural or extrascriptural doctrines, resulting in stunted growth and retarded development. It is little less than stark tragedy that an individual Christian may pass from youth to old age in a state of suspended growth and all his life be unaware of it. Those who would question the truth of this have only to read the First Epistle to the Corinthians and the Book of Hebrews. And even a slight acquaintance with church history will add all the further proof that is needed. Today there exist in the world certain Christian bodies whose histories date far back. These have perpetuated themselves after their kind for hundreds of years, but they have managed to produce nothing but weak, stunted Christians, if Christians they can be called. Common charity forbids that we identify these by name, but any enlightened believer will understand.

Evangelicalism as we know it today in its various manifestations *does* produce some real Christians. We have no wish to question this; we desire rather to assert it unequivocally. But the spiritual climate into which many modern Christians are born does not make for vigorous spiritual growth. Indeed, the whole evangelical world is to a large extent unfavorable to healthy Christianity. And I am not thinking of Modernism either. I mean rather the Bible-believing crowd that bears the name of orthodoxy.

We may as well face it: the whole level of spirituality among us is low. We have measured ourselves by ourselves until the incentive to seek higher plateaus in the things of the Spirit is all but gone. Large and influential sections of the world of fundamental Christianity have gone overboard for practices wholly unscriptural, altogether unjustifiable in the light of historic Christian truth and deeply damaging to the inner life of the individual Christian. They have imitated the world, sought popular favor, manufactured delights to substitute for the joy of the Lord and produced a cheap and synthetic power to substitute for the power of the Holy Ghost. The glowworm has taken the place of the bush that burned and scintillating personalities now answer to the fire that fell at Pentecost.

The fact is that we are not today producing saints. We are making converts to an effete type of Christianity that bears little resemblance to that of the New Testament. The average so-called Bible Christian in our times is but a wretched parody on true sainthood. Yet we put millions of dollars behind movements to perpetuate this degenerate form of religion and attack the man who dares to challenge the wisdom of it.

Clearly we must begin to produce better Christians. We must insist on New Testament sainthood for our converts, nothing less; and we must lead them into a state of heart purity, fiery love, separation from the world and poured-out devotion to the Person of Christ. Only in this way can the low level of spirituality be raised again to where it should be in the light of the Scriptures and of eternal values.

We Need Men of God Again

THE CHURCH at this moment needs men, the right kind of men, bold men. The talk is that we need revival, that we need a new baptism of the Spirit—and God knows we must have both; but God will not revive mice. He will not fill rabbits with the Holy Ghost.

We languish for men who feel themselves expendable in the warfare of the soul, who cannot be frightened by threats of death because they have already died to the allurements of this world. Such men will be free from the compulsions that control weaker men. They will not be forced to do things by the squeeze of circumstances; their only compulsion will come from within—or from above.

This kind of freedom is necessary if we are to have prophets in our pulpits again instead of mascots. These free men will serve God and mankind from motives too high to be understood by the rank and file of religious retainers who today shuttle in and out of the sanctuary. They will make no decisions out of fear, take no course out of a desire to please, accept no service for financial considerations, perform no religious act out of mere custom; nor will they allow themselves to be influenced by the love of publicity or the desire for reputation.

Much that the church—even the evangelical church—is doing these days she is doing because she is afraid not to. Ministerial associations take up projects for no higher reason than that they are being scared into it. Whatever their ear-to-the-ground, fear-inspired reconnoitering leads them to believe the world expects them to do they will be doing come next Monday morning with all kinds of trumped-up zeal and show of godliness. The pressure of public opinion calls these prophets, not the voice of Jehovah.

The true church has never sounded out public expectations before launching her cruasdes. Her leaders heard from God and went ahead wholly independent of popular support or the lack of it. They knew their Lord's will and did it, and their people followed them—sometimes to triumph, oftener to insults and public persecution—and their sufficient reward was the satisfaction of being right in a wrong world.

Another characteristic of the true prophet has been love. The free man who has learned to hear God's voice and dared to obey it has felt the moral burden that broke the hearts of the Old Testament prophets, crushed the soul of our Lord Jesus Christ and wrung streams of tears from the eyes of the apostles.

The free man has never been a religious tyrant, nor has he sought to lord it over God's heritage. It is fear and lack of self-assurance that has led men to try to crush others under their feet. These have had some interest to protect, some position to secure, so they have demanded subjection from their followers as a guarantee of their own safety. But the free man—never; he has nothing to protect, no ambition to pursue and no enemy to fear. For that reason he is completely careless of his standing among men. If they follow him, well and good; if not, he loses nothing that he holds dear; but whether he is accepted or rejected he will go on loving his people with sincere devotion. And only death can silence his tender intercession for them.

Yes, if evangelical Christianity is to stay alive she must have men again, the right kind of men. She must repudiate the weaklings who dare not speak out, and she must seek in prayer and much humility the coming again of men of the stuff prophets and martyrs are made of. God will hear the cries of His people as He heard the cries of Israel in Egypt. And He will send deliverance by sending deliverers. It is His way among men.

And when the deliverers come—reformers, revivalists, prophets—they will be men of God and men of courage. They will have God on their side because they will be careful to stay on God's side. They will be co-workers with Christ and instruments in the hand of the Holy Ghost. Such men will be baptized with the Spirit indeed, and through their labors He will baptize others and send the long delayed revival.

New Spiritual Leadership Imperative

SOMEONE WROTE the godly Macarius of Optino that his spiritual counsel had been helpful.

"This cannot be," Macarius wrote in reply. "Only the mistakes are mine. All good advice is the advice of the Spirit of God; His advice that I happen to have heard rightly and to have passed on without distorting it."

There is an excellent lesson here which we must not allow to go unregarded. It is the sweet humility of the man of God. "Only the mistakes are mine." He was fully convinced that his own efforts could result only in mistakes, and that any good that came of his advice must be the work of the Holy Spirit operating within him. Apparently this was more than a sudden impulse of self-depreciation, which the proudest of men may at times feel; it was rather a settled conviction with him, a conviction that gave set and direction to his entire life. His long and humble ministry which brought spiritual aid to multitudes of persons reveals this clearly enough.

In this day when shimmering personalities carry on the Lord's work after the methods of the entertainment world it is refreshing to associate for a moment even in the pages of a book with a sincere and humble man who keeps his own personality out of sight and places the emphasis upon the inworking of God. It is our belief that the evangelical movement will continue to drift farther and farther from the New Testament position unless its leadership passes from the modern religious star to the self-effacing saint who asks for no praise and seeks no place, happy only when the glory is attributed to God and himself forgotten.

Until such men as these return again to spiritual leadership we may expect a progressive deterioration in the quality of popular Christianity year after year till we reach the point where the grieved Holy Spirit withdraws like the Shekinah from the temple and we are left like Jerusalem after the crucifixion, God-deserted and alone. In spite of every effort to torture doctrine to prove that the Spirit will not forsake religious men, the record reveals plainly enough that He sometimes does. He has in the past forsaken groups when they have gone too far to make a recovery.

It is an open question whether or not the evangelical movement has sinned too long and departed too far from God to return again to spiritual sanity. Personally I do not believe it is too late to repent if the Christians of the day would repudiate evil leadership and seek God again in true penitence and tears. The *if* is the big problem. Will they? Or are they too well satisfied with religious frolic and froth even to recognize their sad departure from the New Testament faith? If the latter is true, then there is nothing left but judgment.

The devil is adept at the use of the red herring. He knows well how to divert the attention of the praying Christian from his subtler but deadly attacks to something more obvious and less harmful. Then while the soldiers of the Lord gather excitedly at one gate he quietly enters by another. And when the saints lose interest in the red herring they return to find the newly baptized and pious enemy in charge of proceedings. So far are they from recognizing him that they soon adopt his ways and call it progress.

Within the last quarter of a century we have actually seen a major shift in the beliefs and practices of the evangelical wing of the church so radical as to amount to a complete sellout; and all this behind the cloak of fervent orthodoxy. With Bibles under their arms and bundles of tracts in their pockets, religious persons now meet to carry on "services" so carnal, so pagan, that they can hardly be distinguished from the old vaudeville shows of earlier days. And for a preacher or a writer to challenge this heresy is to invite ridicule and abuse from every quarter.

Our only hope is that renewed spiritual pressure will be exerted increasingly by self-effacing and courageous men who desire nothing but the glory of God and the purity of the church. May God send us many of them. They are long overdue.

The Gift of Prophetic Insight

A PROPHET IS one who knows his times and what God is trying to say to the people of his times.

What God says to His church at any given period depends altogether upon her moral and spiritual condition and upon the spiritual need of the hour. Religious leaders who continue mechanically to expound the Scriptures without regard to the current religious situation are no better than the scribes and lawyers of Jesus' day who faithfully parroted the Law without the remotest notion of what was going on around them spiritually. They fed the same diet to all and seemed wholly unaware that there was such a thing as meat in due season. The prophets never made that mistake nor wasted their efforts in that manner. They invariably spoke to the condition of the people of their times.

Today we need prophetic preachers; not preachers of prophecy merely, but preachers with a gift of prophecy. The word of wisdom is missing. We need the gift of discernment again in our pulpits. It is not ability to predict that we need, but the anointed eye, the power of spiritual penetration and interpretation, the ability to appraise the religious scene as viewed from God's position, and to tell us what is actually going on.

There has probably never been another time in the history of the world when so many people knew so much about religious happenings as they do today. The newspapers are eager to print religious news; the secular news magazines devote several pages of each issue to the doings of the church and the synagogue; a number of press associations gather church news and make it available to the religious journals at a small cost. Even the hiring of professional publicity men to plug one or another preacher or religious movement is no longer uncommon; the mails are stuffed with circulars and "releases," while radio and television join to tell the listening public what religious people are doing throughout the world.

Greater publicity for religion may be well and I have no fault to find with it. Surely religion should be the most newsworthy thing on earth, and there may be some small encouragement in the thought that vast numbers of persons want to read about it. What disturbs me is that amidst all the religious hubbub hardly a voice is raised to tell us what God thinks about the whole thing.

Where is the man who can see through the ticker tape and confetti to discover which way the parade is headed, why it started in the first place and, particularly, who is riding up front in the seat of honor?

Not the fact that the churches are unusually active these days, not what religious people are doing, should engage our attention, but *why* these things are so. The big question is *Why?* And no one seems to have an answer for it. Not only is there no answer, but scarcely is there anyone to ask the question. It just never occurs to us that such a question remains to be asked. Christian people continue to gossip religious shoptalk with scarcely as much as a puzzled look. The soundness of current Christianity is assumed by the religious masses as was the soundness of Judaism when Christ appeared. People know they are seeing certain activity, but just what it means they do not know, nor have they the faintest idea of where God is or what relation He has toward the whole thing.

What is needed desperately today is prophetic insight. Scholars can interpret the past; it takes prophets to interpret the present. Learning will enable a man to pass judgment on our yesterdays, but it requires a gift of clear seeing to pass sentence on our own day. One hundred years from now historians will know what was taking place religiously in this year of our Lord; but that will be too late for us. We should know right now.

If Christianity is to receive a rejuvenation it must be by other means than any now being used. If the church in the second half of this century is to recover from the injuries she suffered in the first half, there must appear a new type of preacher. The proper, ruler-of-the-synagogue type will never do. Neither will the priestly type of man who carries out his duties, takes his pay and asks no questions, nor the smooth-talking pastoral type who knows how to make the Christian religion acceptable to everyone. All these have been tried and found wanting.

Another kind of religious leader must arise among us. He must be of the old prophet type, a man who has seen visions of God and has heard a voice from the Throne. When he comes (and I pray God there will be not one but many) he will stand in flat contradiction to everything our smirking, smooth civilization holds dear. He will contradict, denounce and protest in the name of God and will earn the hatred and opposition of a large segment of Christendom. Such a man is likely to be lean, rugged, blunt-spoken and a little bit angry with the world. He will love Christ and the souls of men to the point of willingness to die for the glory of the one and the salvation of the other. But he will fear nothing that breathes with mortal breath.

We need to have the gifts of the Spirit restored again to the church, and it is my belief that the one gift we need most now is the gift of prophecy.

The Prophet Is a Man Apart

THE CHURCH IS God's witness to each generation, and her ministers are her voice. Through them she becomes vocal. By them she has spoken always to the world, and by them God has spoken to the church herself. The testimony of her godly laymen has ever been a mighty aid in the work she seeks to accomplish. But her laymen can never do, and assuredly are not called to do, the work of her ministers. By gift and calling the minister is a man apart.

It is not enough, however, that the man of God preach the truth. He has no right to take up a man's time telling him what is true merely. It is a doubtful compliment to any preacher to nod the head and say, "That is true." The same might properly be said if he were doing no more than reciting the multiplication table. It also is true.

A church can wither as surely under the ministry of soulless Bible exposition as it can where no Bible at all is given. To be effective the preacher's message must be alive; it must alarm, arouse, challenge; it must be God's present voice to a particular people.

Then, and not till then, is it the prophetic word and the man himself a prophet.

To fulfill perfectly his calling the prophet must be under the constant sway of the Holy Ghost; and further, he must be alert to moral and spiritual conditions. All spiritual teaching should be related to life. It should intrude into the daily and private living of the hearers. Without being personal, the true prophet will yet pierce the conscience of each listener as if the message had been directed to him alone.

Really to preach the truth it is often necessary that the man of God know the people's hearts better than they themselves do. People are frequently confused and inwardly at cross-purposes. The anointed prophet must speak to this confusion with clarifying wisdom. He must surprise his hearers with his unsuspected knowledge of their secret thoughts.

The work of a minister is, in fine, altogether too difficult for any man. He is driven to God for wisdom. He must seek the mind of Christ and throw himself on the Holy Spirit for spiritual power and mental acumen equal to the task.

Exposition Must Have Application

CHARLES G. FINNEY believed that Bible teaching without moral application could be worse than no teaching at all and could result in positive injury to the hearers. I used to feel that this might be an extreme position, but after years of observation I have come around to it, or to a view almost identical with it.

There is scarcely anything so dull and meaningless as Bible doctrine taught for its own sake. Truth divorced from life is not truth in its Biblical sense, but something else and something less. Theology is a set of facts concerning God, man and the world. These facts may be and often are set forth as values in themselves; and there lies the snare both for the teacher and for the hearer.

The Bible is among other things a book of revealed truth. That is, certain facts are revealed that could not be discovered by the most brilliant mind. These facts are of such a nature as to be past finding out. They were hidden behind a veil, and until certain men who spoke as they were moved by the Holy Ghost took away that veil no mortal man could know them. This lifting of the veil of unknowing from undiscoverable things we call divine revelation.

The Bible, however, is more than a volume of hitherto unknown facts about God, man and the universe. It is a book of exhortation based upon those facts. By far the greater portion of the book is devoted to an urgent effort to persuade people to alter their ways and bring their lives into harmony with the will of God as set forth in its pages.

No man is better for knowing that God in the beginning created the heaven and the earth. The devil knows that, and so did Ahab and Judas Iscariot. No man is better for knowing that God so loved the world of men that He gave His only begotten Son to die for their redemption. In hell there are millions who know that. Theological truth is useless until it is obeyed. The purpose behind all doctrine is to secure moral action.

What is generally overlooked is that truth as set forth in the Christian Scriptures is a moral thing; it is not addressed to the intellect only, but to the will also. It addresses itself to the total man, and its obligations cannot be discharged by grasping it mentally. Truth engages the citadel of the human heart and is not satisfied until it has conquered everything there. The will must come forth and surrender its sword. It must stand at attention to receive orders, and those orders it must joyfully obey. Short of this any knowledge of Christian truth is inadequate and unavailing.

Bible exposition without moral application raises no opposition. It is only when the hearer is made

to understand that truth is in conflict with his heart
that resistance sets in. As long as people can hear
orthodox truth divorced from life they will attend
and support churches and institutions without ob-
jection. The truth is a lovely song, become sweet
by long and tender association; and since it asks
nothing but a few dollars, and offers good music,
pleasant friendships and a comfortable sense of well-
being, it meets with no resistance from the faithful.
Much that passes for New Testament Christianity is
little more than objective truth sweetened with song
and made palatable by religious entertainment.

Probably no other portion of the Scriptures can
compare with the Pauline Epistles when it comes
to making artificial saints. Peter warned that the
unlearned and the unstable would wrest Paul's writings to their own destruction, and we have only
to visit the average Bible conference and listen to
a few lectures to know what he meant. The ominous
thing is that the Pauline doctrines may be taught
with complete faithfulness to the letter of the text
without making the hearers one whit the better.
The teacher may and often does so teach the truth
as to leave the hearers without a sense of moral
obligation.

One reason for the divorce between truth and
life may be lack of the Spirit's illumination. Another surely is the teacher's unwillingness to get
himself into trouble. Any man with fair pulpit
gifts can get on with the average congregation
if he just "feeds" them and lets them alone. Give

them plenty of objective truth and never hint that they are wrong and should be set right, and they will be content.

On the other hand, the man who preaches truth and applies it to the lives of his hearers will feel the nails and the thorns. He will lead a hard life, but a glorious one. May God raise up many such prophets. The church needs them badly.

Christ's Words Are for Christians

THE TALK IS now that if the world is to escape near or total annihilation it must turn for help to the ethics of Jesus. The argument runs something like this:

Within the last century man has leaped ahead in scientific achievement but has lagged behind morally, with the result that he is now technically capable of destroying the world and morally incapable of restraining himself from doing so. Unless the nations of the earth become imbued with the spirit of peace and good will it is highly probable that some trigger-happy politician will fire his shiny new rifle into the ammunition dump and blow up the world.

Because the dump is stored with nuclear explosives any humans who chance to escape the big blow will go out to propagate a race of subhuman mutants, hairless, toothless and deformed. The boys who draw the horror comics enable us to visualize those tragic victims of strontium 90 centuries hence clawing through the twisted rubble of what was once New York or London, emitting simian grunts, wholly unaware of the meaning of the bits of history they pick up and toss impatiently away.

No one with a trace of human pity can think of the effects of nuclear warfare without feeling utter abhorrence for such a thing and deepest compassion for those who may sometime be caught in its fiery hell. In it man's age-old inhumanity to man will have through the ingenuity of modern science surely reached the peak of all possible frightfulness.

Yet we Christians would be foolish to allow ourselves to be carried away by the ominous predictions of unbelieving men. We know well enough that nuclear energy is theoretically capable of wiping out every form of life on this planet, including mankind. *But we also know that such a catastrophe will never occur.* We further know that the earth will never be inhabited by a degenerate race of off-human mutants made so by huge overdoses of radiation.

First, the Holy Scriptures tell us what we could never learn any other way: They tell us what we are, who we are, how we got here, why we are here and what we are required to do while we remain here. They trace our history from the beginning down to the present time and on into the centuries and millenniums ahead. They track us into the atomic age, through the space age and on into the golden age. They reveal that at an appropriate time the direction of the world will be taken away from men and placed in the hands of the Man who alone has the wisdom and power to rule it.

I omit here purposely the details. These are given in satisfying fullness in the writings of the holy prophets and apostles and in the words of Christ spoken while He was yet among us. The one great truth I would emphasize here is that after the war lords have shot their last missile and dropped their last bomb *there will still be living men inhabiting this globe*. After the world has gone through the meat grinder of Armageddon the earth will still be inhabited by men; not by biological freaks, but by real people like you and me.

If the world can escape annihilation only by adopting the ethics of Jesus we may as well resign ourselves to the inevitable explosion, for a huge block of the earth's population is controlled by Communists whose basic ideology is violently anti-Christian and who are determined to extirpate every trace of Christianity from among them. Other large blocks are non-Christian and grimly set to remain so. The West, it is true, pays lips service to Christianity, but selfishness, greed, ambition, pride and lust rule the rulers of these lands almost to a man. While they will now and then speak well of Christ, yet the total quality of their conduct leaves little doubt that they are not much influenced by His teachings.

All this being true, still we Christians can sing at the foot of the threatening volcano. Things have not gotten out of hand. However bad they look, the Lord sitteth king forever and reigneth over the affairs of men. He makes the wrath of man to praise Him and the remainder of wrath He will restrain.

The hope that the nations will accept the ethics of Jesus, disarm and live like brothers is utterly unrealistic and naïve. In the first place, the teachings of Jesus were never intended for the nations of the world. Our Lord sent His followers into all the world to make and baptize disciples. These disciples were to be taught to observe the commandments of Christ. They would thus become a minority group, a peculiar people, in the world but not of it, sometimes tolerated but more often despised and persecuted. And history demonstrates that this is exactly what happened wherever groups of people took the gospel seriously.

To expect of once-born nations conduct possible only to the regenerated, purified, Spirit-led followers of Christ is to confuse the truth of Christianity and hope for the impossible. In the Scriptures the nations of the earth are symbolized by the lion, the bear and the leopard. Christians, in sharp contrast, are likened to peaceful sheep in the midst of wolves, who manage to stay alive only by keeping close to the Shepherd. If the sheep will not act like the bear why should we expect the bear to act like the sheep?

It might be well for us Christians to listen less to the news commentators and more to the voice of the Spirit. And the inspired prophets will prove a fine antidote to the uninspired scientists.

The First Obligation of the Church

THE FIRST LOOK of the church is toward Christ, who is her Head, her Lord and her All.

After that she must be self-regarding and world-regarding, with a proper balance between the two.

By self-regarding I do not mean self-centered. I mean that the church must examine herself constantly to see if she be in the faith; she must engage in severe self-criticism with a cheerful readiness to make amends; she must live in a state of perpetual penitence, seeking God with her whole heart; she must constantly check her life and conduct against the Holy Scriptures and bring her life into line with the will of God.

By world-regarding I mean that the church must know why she is here on earth; that she must acknowledge her indebtedness to all mankind (Rom. 1: 14, 15); that she must take seriously the words of her Lord, "Go ye into all the world, and preach the gospel to every creature" and "Ye shall be witnesses unto me both in Jerusalem, and in all Judaea, and in Samaria, and unto the uttermost part of the earth."

The task of the church is twofold: to spread Christianity throughout the world and to make sure that the Christianity she spreads is the pure New Testament kind.

Theoretically the seed, being the Word of God, should produce the same kind of fruit regardless of the spiritual condition of those who scatter it; but it does not work that way. The identical message preached to the heathen by men of differing degrees of godliness will produce different kinds of converts and result in a quality of Christianity varying according to the purity and power of those who preach it.

Christianity will always reproduce itself after its kind. A worldly-minded, unspiritual church, when she crosses the ocean to give her witness to peoples of other tongues and other cultures, is sure to bring forth on other shores a Christianity much like her own.

Not the naked Word only but the character of the witness determines the quality of the convert. The church can do no more than transplant herself. What she is in one land she will be in another. A crab apple does not become a Grimes Golden by being carried from one country to another. God has written His law deep into all life; everything must bring forth after its kind.

The popular notion that the first obligation of the church is to spread the gospel to the uttermost parts of the earth is false. *Her first obligation is to be spiritually worthy to spread it.* Our Lord said "Go ye," but He also said "Tarry ye," and the tarrying had to come before the going. Had the disciples gone forth as missionaries before the day of Pentecost it would have been an overwhelming spiritual disaster, for they could have done no more than make converts after their own likeness, and this would have altered for the worse the whole history of the Western world and had consequences throughout the ages to come.

To spread an effete, degenerate brand of Christianity to pagan lands is not to fulfill the commandment of Christ or discharge our obligation to the heathen. These terrible words of Jesus haunt my soul: "Ye compass sea and land to make one proselyte, and when he is made, ye make him twofold more the child of hell than yourselves."

To win men to Judaism from among the Gentile nations was altogether a good and right thing to do. Thousands of happy converts were won to the religion of Moses during the years of Israel's spiritual ascendancy, but at the time of Christ Judaism had sunk so low that her missionary effort wrought actual harm instead of good.

It would appear logical that a subnormal, powerless church would not engage in missionary activity, but again the facts contradict the theory. Christian groups that have long ago lost every trace of moral fire nevertheless continue to grow at home and reproduce themselves in other lands. Indeed there is scarcely a fringe sect or heretical cult these days but is enjoying amazing success among the backward peoples of the world.

The evangelical wing of the church has in recent years become world-regarding to a remarkable degree. Within the last twenty years evangelical missionary activity on foreign fields has been stepped up tremendously. But there is in the whole thing one dangerous weakness. That weakness is the naïve assumption that we have only to reach the last tribe with our brand of Christianity and the world has been evangelized. This is an assumption that we dare not make.

Evangelical Christianity is now tragically below the New Testament standard. Worldliness is an accepted part of our way of life. Our religious mood is social instead of spiritual. We have lost the art of worship. We are not producing saints. Our models are successful businessmen, celebrated athletes and theatrical personalities. We carry on our religious activities after the methods of the modern advertiser. Our homes have been turned into theaters. Our literature is shallow and our hymnody borders on sacrilege. And scarcely anyone appears to care.

We must have a better kind of Christian soon or

within another half century we may have no true Christianity at all. Increased numbers of demi-Christians is not enough. We must have a reformation.

The Cross Does Interfere

"THINGS HAVE COME to a pretty pass," said a famous Englishman testily, "when religion is permitted to interfere with our private lives."

To which we may reply that things have come to a worse pass when an intelligent man living in a Protestant country could make such a remark. Had this man never read the New Testament? Had he never heard of Stephen? or Paul? or Peter? Had he never thought about the millions who followed Christ cheerfully to violent death, sudden or lingering, because they *did* allow their religion to interfere with their private lives?

But we must leave this man to his conscience and his Judge and look into our own hearts. Maybe he but expressed openly what some of us feel secretly. Just how radically has our religion interfered with the neat pattern of our own lives? Perhaps we had better answer that question first.

I have long believed that a man who spurns the Christian faith outright is more respected before God and the heavenly powers than the man who pretends to religion but refuses to come under its total domination. The first is an overt enemy, the second a false friend. It is the latter who will be spued out of the mouth of Christ; and the reason is not hard to understand.

One picture of a Christian is a man carrying a cross. "If any man will come after me, let him deny himself, and take up his cross, and follow me." The man with a cross no longer controls his destiny; he lost control when he picked up his cross. That cross immediately became to him an all-absorbing interest, an overwhelming interference. No matter what he may desire to do, there is but one thing he *can* do; that is, move on toward the place of crucifixion.

The man who will not brook interference is under no compulsion to follow Christ. "If any man will," said our Lord, and thus freed every man and placed the Christian life in the realm of voluntary choice.

Yet no man can escape interference. Law, duty, hunger, accident, natural disasters, illness, death, all intrude into his plans, and in the long run there is nothing he can do about it. Long experience with the rude necessities of life has taught men that these interferences will be thrust upon them sooner or later, so they learn to make what terms they can with the inevitable. They learn how to stay within the narrow circular rabbit path where the least interference is to be found. The bolder ones may challenge the world, enlarge the circle somewhat and so increase the number of their problems, but no one invites trouble deliberately. Human nature is not built that way.

Truth is a glorious but hard mistress. She never consults, bargains or compromises. She cries from the top of the high places, "Receive my instruction, and not silver; and knowledge rather than choice gold." After that, every man is on his own. He may accept or refuse, receive or set at naught as he pleases; and there will be no attempt at coercion, though the man's whole destiny is at stake.

Let a man become enamored of Eternal Wisdom and set his heart to win her and he takes on himself a full-time, all-engaging pursuit. Thereafter he will have room for little else. Thereafter his whole life will be filled with seekings and findings, self-repudiations, tough disciplines and daily dyings as he is being crucified unto the world and the world unto him.

Were this an unfallen world the path of truth would be a smooth and easy one. Had the nature of man not suffered a huge moral dislocation there would be no discord between the way of God and the way of man. I assume that in heaven the angels live through a thousand serene millenniums without feeling the slightest discord between their desires and the will of God. But not so among men on earth. Here the natural man receives not the things of the Spirit of God; the flesh lusts against the Spirit and the Spirit against the flesh, and these are contrary one to the other. In that contest there can be only one outcome. We must surrender and God must have His way. His glory and our eternal welfare require that it be so.

Another reason that our religion must interfere with our private lives is that we live in the world, the Bible name for human society. The regenerated man has been inwardly separated from society as Israel was separated from Egypt at the crossing of the Red Sea. The Christian is a man of heaven temporarily living on earth. Though in spirit divided from the race of fallen men he must yet in the flesh live among them. In many things he is like them, but in others he differs so radically from them that they cannot but see and resent it. From the days of Cain and Abel the man of earth has punished the man of heaven for being different. The long history of persecution and martyrdom confirms this.

But we must not get the impression that the Christian life is one continuous conflict, one unbroken irritating struggle against the world, the flesh and the devil. A thousand times no. The heart that learns to die with Christ soon knows the blessed experience of rising with Him, and all the world's persecutions cannot still the high note of holy joy that springs up in the soul that has become the dwelling place of the Holy Spirit.

Each His Own Cross

AN EARNEST CHRISTIAN woman sought help from Henry Suso concerning her spiritual life. She had been imposing rigid austerities upon herself in an effort to feel the sufferings that Christ had felt on the cross. Things weren't going so well with her and Suso knew why.

The old saint wrote his spiritual daughter and reminded her that our Lord had not said, "If any man will come after me, let him deny himself, and take up *my* cross, and follow me." He had said, "Let him . . . take up *his* cross." There is a difference of only one small pronoun; but that difference is vast and important.

Crosses are all alike, but no two are identical. Never before nor since has there been a cross-experience just like that endured by the Saviour. The whole dreadful work of dying which Christ suffered was something unique in the experience of mankind. It had to be so if the cross was to mean life for the world. The sin-bearing, the darkness, the rejection by the Father were agonies peculiar to the Person of the holy sacrifice. To claim any experience remotely like that of Christ would be more than an error; it would be sacrilege.

Every cross was and is an instrument of death, but no man could die on the cross of another; each man died on his own cross; hence Jesus said, "Let him . . . take up *his* cross, and follow me."

Now there is a real sense in which the cross of Christ embraces all crosses and the death of Christ encompasses all deaths. "If one died for all, then were all dead" . . . "I am crucified with Christ" . . . "The cross of our Lord Jesus Christ, by whom the world is crucified unto me, and I unto the world." This is in the judicial working of God in redemption. The Christian as a member of the body of Christ is crucified along with his divine Head. Before God every true believer is reckoned to have died when Christ died. All subsequent experience of personal crucifixion is based upon this identification with Christ on the cross.

But in the practical, everyday outworking of the believer's crucifixion his own cross is brought into play. "Let him . . . take up *his* cross." That is obviously not the cross of Christ. Rather it is the believer's own personal cross by means of which the cross of Christ is made effective in slaying his evil nature and setting him free from its power.

The believer's own cross is one he has assumed voluntarily. Therein lies the difference between his cross and the cross on which Roman convicts died. They went to the cross against their will; he, because he chooses to do so. No Roman officer ever pointed to a cross and said, "If any man will, let him." Only Christ said that, and by so saying He placed the whole matter in the hands of the Christian. He can refuse to take his cross, or he can stoop and take it up and start for the dark hill. The difference between great sainthood and spiritual mediocrity depends upon which choice he makes.

To go along with Christ step by step and point by point in identical suffering of Roman crucifixion is not possible for any of us, and certainly is not intended by our Lord. What He does intend is that each of us should count himself dead indeed with Christ, and then accept willingly whatever of self-denial, repentance, humility and humble sacrifice that may be found in the path of obedient daily living. That is *his* cross, and it is the only one the Lord has invited him to bear.

Holiness Before Happiness

A SELFISH DESIRE for happiness is as sinful as any other selfish desire. Its root is in the flesh which can never have any standing before God. "The carnal mind is enmity against God: for it is not subject to the law of God, neither indeed can be" (Rom. 8: 7).

People are coming more and more to excuse every sort of wrongdoing on the grounds that they are "just trying to secure a little happiness." Before she will give her consent to marriage the modern young lady may ask outright whether or not the man "can make me happy," instead of wondering selflessly whether she can bring happiness to her life partner. The lovelorn columns of the newspapers are wet with the self-pitying tears of persons who write to inquire how they can "preserve their happiness." The psychiatrists of the land are getting fat off the increasing numbers who seek professional aid in their all-absorbing search for happiness. It is not uncommon for crimes to be committed against persons who do nothing worse than "jeopardize" someone's happiness.

That is the hedonistic philosophy of old Grecian days misunderstood and applied to everyday living in the twentieth century. It destroys all nobility of character and makes milksops of all who consciously or unconsciously adopt it; but it has become quite the popular creed of the masses. That we are born to be happy is scarcely questioned by anyone. No one bothers to prove that fallen men have any moral right to happiness, or that they are in the long run any better off happy. The only question before the house is how to get the most happiness out of life. Almost all popular books and plays assume that personal happiness is the legitimate end of the dramatic human struggle.

Now I submit that the whole hectic scramble after

happiness is an evil as certainly as is the scramble after money or fame or success. It springs out of a vast misunderstanding of ourselves and of our true moral state. The man who really knows himself can never believe in his right to be happy. A little glimpse of his own heart will disillusion him instantly so that he is more likely to turn on himself and own God's sentence against him to be just. The doctrine of man's inalienable right to happiness is anti-God and anti-Christ, and its wide acceptance by society tells us a lot about that same society.

The effect of this modern hedonism is felt also among the people of God. The gospel is too often presented as a means toward happiness, to peace of mind or security. There are even those who use the Bible to "relax" them, as if it were a drug.

How far wrong all this is will be discovered easily by the simple act of reading the New Testament through once with meditation. There the emphasis is not upon happiness but upon holiness. God is more concerned with the state of people's hearts than with the state of their feelings. Undoubtedly the will of God brings final happiness to those who obey, but the most important matter is not how happy we are but how holy. The soldier does not seek to be happy in the field; he seeks rather to get the fighting over with, to win the war and get back home to his loved ones. There he may enjoy himself to the full; but while the war is on his most pressing job is to be a good soldier, to acquit himself like a man, regardless of how he feels.

The childish clamor after happiness can become a real snare. One may easily deceive himself by cultivating a religious joy without a correspondingly righteous life. No man should desire to be happy who is not at the same time holy. He should spend his efforts in seeking to know and do the will of God, leaving to Christ the matter of how happy he shall be.

For those who take this whole thing seriously I have a suggestion: Go to God and have an understanding. Tell Him that it is your desire to be holy at any cost and then ask Him never to give you more happiness than holiness. When your holiness becomes tarnished, let your joy become dim. And ask Him to make you holy whether you are happy or not. Be assured that in the end you will be as happy as you are holy; but for the time being let your whole ambition be to serve God and be Christlike.

If we dare to take a stand like that we may expect to know a new degree of inward purification. And, God being who He is, we are more than likely to know a new degree of happiness as well, but a happiness that springs out of a more intimate fellowship with God, a happiness that is elevated and unselfish and free from the pollutions of the flesh.

The Need for Self-judgment

BETWEEN DEEDS AND consequences there is a relationship as close and inescapable as that which exists between the seed and the harvest.

We are moral beings and as such we must accept the consequence of every deed done and every word spoken. We cannot act apart from the concept of right and wrong. By our very nature we are compelled to own a three-dimensional moral obligation every time we exercise the right of choice; namely, the obligation to God, to ourselves and to others. No conscious moral being can be imagined to exist for even one moment in a nonmoral situation.

The whole question of right and wrong, of moral responsibility, of justice and judgment and reward and punishment, is sharply accented for us by the fact that we are members of a fallen race, occupying a position halfway between hell and heaven, with the knowledge of good and evil inherent within our intricate natures, along with ability to turn toward good and an inborn propensity to turn toward evil.

The present state of the human race before God is probationary. The world is on trial. The voice of God sounds over the earth, "Behold I set before you the way of life and the way of death. Choose you this day."

It has been held by most Jews and Christians that the period of probation for the individual ends with his death and after that comes the judgment. This belief is supported completely by the Scriptures of the Old and New Testaments, and any variance from this view is the result of the introduction of non-scriptural religious and philosophical concepts into Christian thinking.

The cross of Christ has altered somewhat the position of certain persons before the judgment of God. Toward those who embrace the provisions of mercy that center around the death and resurrection of Christ one phase of judgment is no longer operative. "He that heareth my word, and believeth on him that sent me, hath everlasting life, and shall not come into condemnation; but is passed from death unto life" (John 5: 24).

That is the way our Lord stated this truth, and we have only to know that the word "condemnation" as it occurs here is actually *judgment* to see that for believers the consequences of sinful deeds have, in at least one aspect, been remitted.

When Christ died in the darkness for us men He made it possible for God to remit the penalty of the broken law, re-establish repentant sinners in His favor exactly as if they had never sinned, and do the whole thing without relaxing the severity of the law or compromising the high demands of justice (Rom. 3: 24-26).

This is a mystery too high for us and we honor God more by believing without understanding than by trying to understand. The Just died for the unjust; and because He did, the unjust may now live with the Just in complete moral congruity. Thanks be to God for His unspeakable gift.

Does this mean that the redeemed man has no responsibility to God for his conduct? Does it mean that now that he is clothed with the righteousness of Christ he will never be called to account for his deeds? God forbid! How could the moral Governor of the universe release a segment of that universe from the moral law of deeds and consequences and hope to uphold the order of the world?

Within the household of God among the redeemed and justified there is law as well as grace; not the law of Moses that knew no mercy, but the kindly law of the Father's heart that requires and expects of His children lives lived in conformity to the commandments of Christ.

If these words should startle anyone, so let it be and more also, for our Lord has told us plainly and has risen up early and sent His apostles to tell us that we must all give account of the deeds done in the body. And He has warned us faithfully of the danger that we shall have for our reward only wood, hay and stubble in the day of Christ (Rom. 14: 7-12, 1 Cor. 3: 9-15).

The judgment unto death and hell lies behind the Christian, but the judgment seat of Christ lies ahead. There the question will not be the law of

Moses, but how we have lived within the Father's household; our record will be examined for evidence of faithfulness, self-discipline, generosity beyond the demands of the law, courage before our detractors, humility, separation from the world, cross-carrying and a thousand little deeds of love that could never occur to the mere legalist or to the unregenerate soul.

"If we would judge ourselves," said Paul when speaking of carnal abuses in the Corinthian church, "we should not be judged." This introduces at least the possibility that we may anticipate the judgment seat of Christ and prepare ourselves against it by honest self-judgment here in this life.

This deserves a lot of prayerful consideration from us. We have the Bible before us and the Holy Spirit within us. What is to hinder us from facing the judgment seat now while we can do something about it?

Prayer No Substitute for Obedience

HAVE YOU NOTICED how much praying for revival has been going on of late—and how little revival has resulted?

Considering the volume of prayer that is ascending these days, rivers of revival should be flowing in blessing throughout the land. That no such results are in evidence should not discourage us; rather it should stir us to find out why our prayers are not answered.

Everything has its proper cause in the Kingdom of God as well as in the natural world. The reason for God's obvious refusal to send revival may lie deep, but surely not too deep to discover.

I believe our problem is that we have been trying to substitute praying for obeying; and it simply will not work.

A church, for instance, follows its traditions without much thought about whether they are scriptural or not. Or it surrenders to pressure from public opinion and falls in with popular trends which carry it far from the New Testament pattern. Then the leaders notice a lack of spiritual power among the people and become concerned about it. What to do? How can they achieve that revitalization of spirit they need so badly? How can they bring down refreshing showers to quicken their fainting souls?

The answer is all ready for them. The books tell them how—pray! The passing evangelist confirms what the books have said—pray! The word is echoed back and forth, growing in volume until it becomes a roar—pray! So the pastor calls his people to prayer. Days and nights are spent begging God to be merciful and send revival upon His people. The tide of feeling runs high and it looks for a while as if the revival might be on the way. But it fails to arrive and the zeal for prayer begins to flag. Soon the church is back where it was before, and a numb discouragement settles over everyone. What has gone wrong?

Simply this: Neither the leaders nor the people have made any effort to obey the Word of God. They felt that their only weakness was failure to pray, when actually in a score of ways they were falling short in the vital matter of obedience. "To obey is better than sacrifice." Prayer is never an ac-acceptable substitute for obedience. The sovereign Lord accepts no offering from His creatures that is not accompanied by obedience. To pray for revival while ignoring or actually flouting the plain precept laid down in the Scriptures is to waste a lot of words and get nothing for our trouble.

It has been quite overlooked in recent times that the faith of Christ is an absolute arbiter. It preempts the whole redeemed personality and seizes upon the individual to the exclusion of all other claims. Or more accurately, it makes every legitimate claim on the Christian's life conditional, and without hesitation decides the place each claim shall have in the total scheme. The act of committal to Christ in salvation releases the believing man from the penalty of sin, but it does not release him from the obligation to obey the words of Christ. Rather it brings him under the joyous necessity to obey.

Look at the epistles of the New Testament and

notice how largely they are given over to what is erroneously called "hortatory" matter. By dividing the epistles into "doctrinal" and "hortatory" passages we have relieved ourselves of any necessity to obey. The doctrinal passages require from us nothing except that we believe them. The so-called hortatory passages are harmless enough, for the very word by which they are described declares them to be words of advice and encouragement rather than commandments to be obeyed. This is a palpable error.

The exhortations in the epistles are to be understood as apostolic injunctions carrying the weight of mandatory charges from the Head of the Church. They are intended to be obeyed, not weighed as bits of good advice which we are at liberty to accept or reject as we will.

If we would have God's blessing upon us we must begin to obey. Prayer will become effective when we stop using it as a substitute for obedience. God will not accept praying in lieu of obeying. We only deceive ourselves when we try to make the substitution.

Not All Faith Pleases God

WITHOUT FAITH IT is impossible to please God, but not all faith pleases God.

I do not recall another period when faith was as popular as it is today. After the first World War the man of faith was considered weak and frightfully behind the intellectual parade. But since the close of World War II the pendulum has swung far in the other direction. Faith has come back into favor with almost everybody. The scientist, the cab driver, the philosopher, the actress, the politician, the prize fighter, the housewife—all are ready to recommend faith as the panacea for all our ills, moral, spiritual and economic.

If we only believe hard enough we'll make it somehow. So goes the popular chant. What you believe is not important. Only believe. Jew, Catholic, nature mystic, deist, occultist, swami, Mormon, Sufi, moon-struck poet without religious convictions, political dreamer or aspirant for a cottage on Uranus or Mars—just keep on believing, and peace, it will be wonderful. Soon a disease-free, warless world will emerge from the mists inhabited by a colorless, creedless, classless race where men will brothers be for a' that and a' that.

Back of this is the nebulous idea that faith is an almighty power flowing through the universe which anyone may plug into at will. It is conceived vaguely as a subrational creative pulsation streaming down from somewhere Up There, ready at any time to enter our hearts and change our whole mental and moral constitution as well as our total outlook on man, God and the cosmos. When it comes in, out go pessimism, fear, defeat and failure; in come optimism, confidence, personal mastery, and unfailing success in war, love, sports, business and politics.

All of this is, of course, a gossamer of self-deception woven of the unsubstantial threads of fancy spun out of minds of tenderhearted persons who want to believe it. It is a kind of poor man's transcendentalism which, in the form we have with us today, came down from the more literary and respectable transcendentalism of the New England of a century ago.

Transcendentalism is a sort of creedless religion, growing out of the will to believe and an unwillingness to believe the Holy Scriptures. To discover the tenets of transcendentalism is extremely difficult, if indeed any such tenets actually exist; but Emerson gave us a hint when he said, "Belief consists in accepting the affirmations of the soul; unbelief, in denying them." I think this may be taken as a fair summary of Emerson's religious belief, and certainly it is an accurate description of the humanistic faith of the quasi-Christian masses today.

What is overlooked in all this is that faith is a good

only when it engages truth; when it is made to rest upon falsehood it can and often does lead to eternal tragedy. For it is not enough that we believe; we must believe the right thing about the right One. To believe in God is more than to believe that He exists. Ahab and Judas believed that. To a right faith knowledge is necessary. We must know at least something of what God is like and what His will is for His human creatures. To know less than this is to be thrown back upon the necessity of accepting the affirmations of the soul and substituting "Thus saith my soul" for the Biblical "Thus saith the Lord."

True faith requires that we believe everything God has said about Himself, but also that we believe everything He has said about *us*. Until we believe that we are as bad as God says we are, we can never believe that He will do for us what He says He will do. Right here is where popular religion breaks down. It never quite accepts the severity of God or the depravity of man. It stresses the goodness of God and man's misfortune. Sin is a pardonable frailty and God is not too much concerned about it. He merely wants us to trust in His goodness.

To believe thus is to ground faith upon falsehood and build our eternal hope upon sand. No man has any right to pick and choose among revealed truths. God has spoken. We are all under solemn obligation to hear the affirmations of the Holy Ghost.

To manipulate the Scriptures so as to make them excuse us, compliment us and console us is to do despite to the written Word and to reject the Living Word. To believe savingly in Jesus Christ is to believe all He has said about Himself and all that the prophets and apostles have said about Him. Let us beware that the Jesus we "accept" is not one we have created out of the dust of our imagination and formed after our own likeness.

True faith commits us to obedience. "We have received grace and apostleship," says Paul, "for obedience to the faith among all nations" (Rom. 1: 5). That dreamy, sentimental faith which ignores the judgments of God against us and listens to the affirmations of the soul is as deadly as cyanide. That faith which passively accepts all the pleasant texts of the Scriptures while it overlooks or rejects the stern warnings and commandments of those same Scriptures is not the faith of which Christ and His apostles spoke.

Faith in faith is faith astray. To hope for heaven by means of such faith is to drive in the dark across a deep chasm on a bridge that doesn't quite reach the other side.

Religion Should Produce Action

THE SUPREME PURPOSE of the Christian religion is to make men like God in order that they may act like God. In Christ the verbs *to be* and *to do* follow each other in that order.

True religion leads to moral action. The only true Christian is the practicing Christian. Such a one is in very reality an incarnation of Christ as Christ is the incarnation of God; not in the same degree and fullness of perfection, for there is nothing in the moral universe equal to that awful mystery of godliness which joined God and man in eternal union in the person of the Man Christ Jesus; but as the fullness of the Godhead was and is in Christ, so Christ is in the nature of the one who believes in Him in the manner prescribed in the Scriptures.

God always acts like Himself wherever He may be and whatever He may be doing. When God became flesh and dwelt among us He did not cease to act as He had been acting from eternity. "He veiled His deity but He did not void it." The ancient flame dimmed down to spare the helpless eyes of mortal men, but as much as was seen was true fire. Christ restrained His powers but He did not violate

His holiness. In whatsoever He did He was holy, harmless, separate from sinners and higher than the highest heaven.

Just as in eternity God acted like Himself and when incarnated in human flesh still continued in all His conduct to be true to His holiness, so does He when He enters the nature of a believing man. This is the method by which He makes the redeemed man holy. He enters a human nature at regeneration as He once entered human nature at the incarnation and acts as becomes God, using that nature as a medium of expression for His moral perfections.

Cicero, the Roman orator, once warned his hearers that they were in danger of making philosophy a substitute for action instead of allowing it to produce action. What is true of philosophy is true also of religion. The faith of Christ was never intended to be an end in itself nor to serve instead of something else. In the minds of some teachers faith stands in lieu of moral conduct and every inquirer after God must take his choice between the two. We are presented with the well-known either/or: either we have faith or we have works, and faith saves while works damn us. Hence the tremendous emphasis on faith and the apologetic, mincing approach to the doctrine of personal holiness in modern evangelism. This error has lowered the moral standards of the church and helped to lead us into the wilderness where we currently find ourselves.

Rightly understood, faith is not a substitute for

moral conduct but a means toward it. The tree does not serve in lieu of fruit but as an agent by which fruit is secured. Fruit, not trees, is the end God has in mind in yonder orchard; so Christ-like conduct is the end of Christian faith. To oppose faith to works is to make the fruit the enemy to the tree; yet that is exactly what we have managed to do. And the consequences have been disastrous.

A miscalculation in laying the foundation of a building will throw the whole superstructure out of plumb, and the error that gave us faith as a sub-stitute for action instead of faith in action has raised up in our day unsymmetrical and ugly temples of which we may well be ashamed and for which we shall surely give a strict account in the day when Christ judges the secrets of our hearts.

In practice we may detect the subtle (and often unconscious) substitution when we hear a Christian assure someone that he will "pray over" his problem, knowing full well that he intends to use prayer as a substitute for service. It is much easier to pray that a poor friend's needs may be supplied than to supply them. James' words burn with irony: "If a brother or sister be naked, and destitute of daily food, and one of you say unto them, Depart in peace, be ye warmed and filled; notwithstanding ye give them not those things which are needful to the body; what doth it profit?" And the mystical John sees also the incongruity involved in substituting religion for ac-tion: "But whoso hath this world's good, and seeth his brother have need, and shutteth up his bowels of compassion from him, how dwelleth the love of God in him? My little children, let us not love in word, neither in tongue; but in deed and in truth. And hereby we know that we are of the truth, and shall assure our hearts before him."

A proper understanding of this whole thing will destroy the false and artificial either/or. Then we will have not less faith but more godly works; not less praying but more serving; not fewer words but more holy deeds; not weaker profession but more courageous possession; not a religion as a substitute for action but religion in faith-filled action.

And what is that but to say that we will have come again to the teaching of the New Testament?

A New Man in an Old World

THE CHRISTIAN WHO has dedicated his life to God and has shouldered his cross need not be surprised at the conflict in which he at once finds himself engaged. Such conflict is logical; it results from the nature of God and of man and of Christianity.

He will, for instance, discover that the ways of God and the ways of men are not equal. He will find that the skills he learned in Adam's world are of very little use to him in the spiritual realm. His tried and proven methods for getting things done will fail him when he attempts to apply them to the work of the Spirit. The new Adam will not surrender to the old Adam nor gear His new creation to the methods of the world. God will not share His glory with another. The seeking Christian must learn the hard way that it is "not by might, nor by power, but by my spirit, saith the Lord of hosts."

The true Church of God, the company of the forgiven and regenerated, is a marvel and an astonishment in the eyes of the old creation. Israel saw the "food of angels" and cried, "What is this?" because it had come down from heaven and was unlike anything with which they were familiar. So they called it "manna," and manna it remained, a wonder among earth's comon things, a perpetual sign of the supernatural in the midst of natural things. The Church is a sheet let down from heaven, an interposition of something unlike and dissimilar, a wonder and a perplexity which cannot be understood nor explained nor gotten rid of. That about her which yields itself to analysis by the historian or the psychologist is the very thing that does not signify, the earthen vessel in which the precious treasure is contained. The treasure itself transcends the art of man to comprehend.

The new Christian is like a man who has learned to drive a car in a country where the traffic moves on the left side of the highway and suddenly finds himself in another country and forced to drive on the right. He must unlearn his old habit and learn a new one and, more serious than all, he must learn in heavy traffic. He must fight his old acquired reflexes and learn new ones, and he has no time or place to practice. He can learn only by driving and the Christian can learn only by living. There is no school of Christianity where the Christian can make his mistakes safely before going out where a mistake will cost him something. The Christian can never afford to be wrong, not even once, though by the good grace of God he can be forgiven if he sins and restored again to fellowship if he does fail his Lord.

Jesus said, "In the world ye shall have tribulation," and Paul reminded us that "all that will live godly in Christ Jesus shall suffer persecution." Among other things, the Bible is a record of the struggle of twice-born men to live in a world run by the once-born. The Psalms and the Prophets are full of the sighs and tears of good men in a bad world, men whose loyalty to the kingdom of heaven was considered treason against the kingdom of man and punished as such. But, as intimated previously, this is not the source of the Christian's most perplexing problem.

Let us get down to cases. A forty-year-old man is suddenly converted to Christ. His conversion is genuine and his inner witness is clear. He is baptized, associates himself with a company of believers in some local church, establishes family prayer, begins to tithe and, up to the light he has, lives as he believes a Christian should. Does that end his problems? Yes and no.

Yes; for him the problem of his past sins is settled. God has wiped the slate clean. He is now a child of God, possessed of eternal life. His past is forgiven, his present in the hands of God and his future guaranteed to him by the blood of the everlasting covenant. That much is sure.

No; for the new world he has entered is altogether different from the one he has just left. Here the moral weather is completely different and he must become acclimated to it. Standards, values, objectives, methods—all are different. Things he had for a lifetime taken for granted are sharply condemned by the Scriptures and by the Holy Spirit within him. He must alter his attitudes toward almost everything. Many solid pillars upon which he had previously leaned without question are now seen to be made of chalk and ready to crumble at any moment. What is worst of all, his self-confidence suddenly vanishes. He sees through the flimsy pretense of the you-can-do-it school of thought. He wonders why Emerson's celebrated essay on Self-Reliance disturbs him now instead of affording him a shot in the arm. He hears the Lord say "Without me ye can do nothing," and falls at His feet like a little child. All the certainty goes out of him and he throws himself out onto the promise of God, every natural hope and every human trust gone forever. This can be a bitter and terrifying experience and it is one, regrettably, that not many persons today know anything about.

If our man follows on to know the Lord he will slowly acquire not only a new philosophy of life but a new set of moral reflexes as well. Old things will pass away and all things will become new. Then he can say with Paul, "I am crucified with Christ: nevertheless I live; yet not I, but Christ liveth in me: and the life I now live in the flesh I live by the faith of the Son of God, who loved me, and gave himself for me" (Gal. 2: 20).

Spiritual Symmetry Is God's Will for Us

SYMMETRY IS A right proportion of parts in relation to each other and to the whole.

By this simple definition symmetry of character is both highly desirable and extremely difficult to attain. Yet it is precisely what Christ had in supreme degree and what every one of us needs if we are to become saints in something beside name.

Emerson said somewhere that nature, when she sets out to make a genius, makes him lopsided in order to achieve some particular effect. Thus a Beethoven must be all ear; a Rembrandt, all eye.

This is so because sin has upset the order of nature and brought discord and disproportion to our lives. For we can hardly conceive of God's creating us in such a way that we should be forced to sacrifice one good thing to attain another. And we cannot imagine that He would be satisfied with lopsided persons, particularly since He at the first made them in His own image. Everything we know about God would dispose us to expect Him to produce beings beautifully proportioned and well adjusted to themselves, with all parts of their complex personalities finely tuned to each other and operating in perfect harmony. Anything less than this would be unworthy of the wisdom and power of God.

If redemption is a moral restoration to the divine image (and it must be that ultimately), then we may expect one of the first acts of God in the Christian's life to be a kind of moral tuning-up, a bringing into harmony the discordant elements within the personality, an adjustment of the soul to itself and to God. And that He does just this is the testimony of everyone who has been truly converted. The new believer may state it in other language and the emotional lift he enjoys may be so great as to prevent calm analysis, but the gist of his testimony will be that he has found peace, a peace he can actually feel. The twists and tensions within his heart have corrected themselves as a result of his new orientation to Christ. He can then sing,

> *"Now rest, my long-divided heart;*
> *Fixed on this blissful center rest."*

But the work of God is not finished when the first act of inward adjustment has been done. The Spirit would go on from there to bring the total life into harmony with that "blissful center." This is wrought in the believer by the Word and by prayer and discipline and suffering. It could be done by a short course in things spiritual if we were more pliable, less self-willed and stubborn; but it usually takes some time before we learn the hard lessons of faith and obedience sufficiently well to permit the work to be done within us with anything near to perfection.

In bringing many sons unto glory God works with whatever He has in whatever way He can and by whatever means He can, respecting always His own gift to us, the freedom of our wills. But of all means He uses the Bible is the best.

The Word of God well understood and religiously obeyed is the shortest route to spiritual perfection. And we must not select a few favorite passages to the exclusion of others. Nothing less than a whole Bible can make a whole Christian. Any tinkering with the truth, any liberties taken with the Scriptures, and we throw ourselves out of symmetry and invite stiff discipline and severe chastisement from that loving Father who wills for us nothing less than full restoration to the image of God in Christ.

Candling Eggs or Feeding Sheep?

SOME TIME AGO I heard a man attempt to pour ridicule upon the custom of pastoral preaching. He didn't believe much in going to church every week to hear the Word of God expounded. He thought it quite unnecessary. After a man is converted he should go out at once and begin to win souls, not go to church and hear preaching.

So argued this good brother, and to prove his point he reasoned that a farmer candles his eggs once, not every week. As soon as the eggs have been candled they are straightway crated and shipped off to market, not taken out the next week and candled again. This all sounded so convincing that one less stubborn might have just surrendered without a fight and handed in his credentials. No more preaching from the pulpit to eggs that had already been candled! The very thought of that farmer candling the same eggs every week would have been too much! Where had I been all my life not to have thought of that before?

But there was one very serious weakness in the argument: Christ did not say to Peter, "Candle my eggs"; He said, "Feed my sheep." Christians are

not eggs to be candled; they are sheep to be fed.
Feeding sheep is not a job to be gotten over with
once and for all; it is a loving act to be repeated at
regular intervals as long as the sheep live. Peter
well understood His Lord's meaning and years later
admonished certain elders of the church to "feed
the flock of God which is among you." Not one
word did he say about candling eggs!

Figures of speech should illustrate truth, not orig-
inate it. Christians are living creatures dependent
upon food, and must be fed well and often if they
are to remain healthy. Our Lord selected the figure
of sheep because it accords with the facts. The
figure of eggs does not.

To contort a fact to make it agree with a figure of
speech is to sin against truth. Truth is sovereign
and will be served by every figure, but it will never
serve any figure, however neat and convincing it
may be.

I once heard a man preach a whole sermon on salt.
He analyzed it chemically, gave a survey of its importance in history, told how it was once used to pay
the Roman soldiers ("*salarium,* from which comes
our English word salary," etc.), and when he was
through with his sermon he had not added one iota
of meaning to the simple words of Jesus, "Ye are the
salt of the earth." Christ knew how to use figures;
some of His followers do not.

Beware the man who makes a figure of speech
teach doctrine. When he begins to draw too many
analogies from a figure, close up on him, for he is

sure to be wrong. And if the Bible does not teach a doctrine do not let a tortured analogy convince you that it does. There's something better in the Bible than figures of speech to be twisted to fit our own prejudices. Let's stick to plain truth, and use figures to illustrate it.

Beware the File-card Mentality

THE ESSENCE OF true religion is spontaneity, the sovereign movings of the Holy Spirit upon and in the free spirit of redeemed men. This has through the years of human history been the hallmark of spiritual excellency, the evidence of reality in a world of unreality.

When religion loses its sovereign character and becomes mere form this spontaneity is lost also, and in its place come precedent, propriety, system—and the file-card mentality.

Back of the file-card mentality is the belief that spirituality can be organized. Then is introduced into religion those ideas which never belong there—numbers, statistics, the law of averages, and other such natural and human things. And creeping death always follows.

Now a file card is a very harmless little tool and a very useful one for some purposes. It is splendid for keeping attendance records in the Sunday school, and a good mailing list can hardly be managed without it. It is a good thing in its place and deadly out of its place. Its danger comes from the well-known human tendency to depend upon external helps in dealing with internal things.

When the file card begins to direct the Christian's life it immediately becomes a nuisance and a curse. When it gets out of the file case and into the human heart, woe be unto us; nothing but an internal spiritual revolution can deliver the victim from his fate.

Here's how the file card works when it gets into the Christian life and begins to create mental habits: It divides the Bible into sections fitted to the days of the year, and compels the Christian to read according to rule. No matter what the Holy Spirit may be trying to say to a man, still he goes on reading where the card tells him, dutifully checking it off each day.

Every Spirit-led saint knows that there are times when he is held by an inward pressure to one chapter, or even one verse, for days at a time while he wrestles with God till some truth does its work within him. To leave that present passage to follow a pre-arranged reading schedule is for him wholly impossible. He is in the hand of the free Spirit, and reality is appearing before him to break and humble and lift and liberate and cheer. But only the free soul can know the glory of this. To this the heart bound by system will be forever a stranger.

The slave to the file card soon finds that his prayers lose their freedom and become less spontaneous, less effective. He finds himself concerned over matters that should give him no concern whatever—how much time he spent in prayer yesterday, whether he did or did not cover his prayer list for the day, whether he gets up as early as he used to do or stays up in prayer as late at night. Inevitably the calendar crowds out the Spirit and the face of the clock hides the face of God. Prayer ceases to be the free breath of a ransomed soul and becomes a duty to be fulfilled. And even if under such circumstances he succeeds in making his prayer amount to something, still he is suffering tragic losses and binding upon his soul a yoke from which Christ died to set him free.

The pastor, too, must watch lest he become the victim of the file card. From the road in, it looks like a good idea to work out a system of sermon coverage, mapping out the doctrines of the Bible as a farmer divides his acres, allowing a certain amount of time during the year for sermons on the various Bible truths so that at the end of a given period proper attention will have been given to each one. Theoretically this should be fine, but it will kill any man who follows it, and it will kill his church as well; and one characteristic of this kind of death is that neither pastor nor people are aware that it has come.

Those responsible for the activities of churches and gospel workers must also look out for the file-card snare. It is a deadly thing and works to quench the spontaneous operation of the Spirit. No one need die, no one need lie in patient, suffering prayer in the presence of God while the Holy Spirit imparts His sovereign will to his believing heart. No vision of God, high and lifted up, no shocking exposure of inner uncleanness, no pain of a burning coal upon the lips.

The glory of the gospel is its freedom. The Pharisees, who were slaves, hated Christ because He was free. The battle for spiritual freedom did not end when our Lord had risen from the dead. It still goes on, and in a tragic degree the sons of freedom are losing it. Many who know better are surrendering their liberties with only a token struggle. They find it easier to consult the card than to pray on to a place of spiritual illumination and inward prophetic assurance.

It will indeed be cause for mourning in Zion when the race of free men dies out in the church and the work of God is entrusted wholly to the file card jockey.

The Evils of a Bad Disposition

A BAD DISPOSITION has been called "the vice of the virtuous." The woman who would not gamble or drink or attend places of worldly amusements may yet manifest a churlish temper and keep her family in terror with her acid tongue. A man who will fight for the faith once delivered to the saints may be so hard to live with that his family actually wishes him gone, and feels little real sorrow when he finally shuffles off this mortal coil to go, as he had fondly believed, to dwell with the saints in the peace of heaven forever.

The slick habit of blaming the devil for conditions in the average church is too smooth to escape suspicion. That explanation explains too much. We do not underestimate the ability of the devil to raise trouble, nor do we believe that he has softened up in his attitude toward the followers of Christ. But his power is specifically limited. It is extremely doubtful whether he has any real power unless we give it to him. At least we know that he could not get to Job without special permission from God, and it is hard to conceive that God took better care of Job than He does of the rest of us. Chrysostom once preached a great sermon to show that nothing can harm a Christian who does not harm himself. Over the humble and obedient soul the devil has no power. He can harm us only when we, by unspiritual and un-Christlike ways, play into his hands. And we play into his hands whenever and as long as we harbor unjudged and uncleansed evil within us.

Dispositional sins are fully as injurious to the Christian cause as the more overt acts of wickedness. These sins are as many as the various facets of human nature. Just so there may be no misunderstanding let us list a few of them: Sensitiveness, irritability, churlishness, faultfinding, peevishness, temper, resentfulness, cruelty, uncharitable attitudes; and of course there are many more. These kill the spirit of the church and slow down any progress which the gospel may be making in the community. Many persons who had been secretly longing to find Christ have been turned away and embittered by manifestations of ugly dispositional flaws in the lives of the very persons who were trying to win them.

Deliverance from inward sins would seem to be a spiritual necessity. In the face of the havoc wrought by dispositional sins among religious people we do not see how sincere men can deny that necessity. Unsaintly saints are the tragedy of Christianity. People of the world usually pass through the circle of disciples to reach Christ, and if they find those disciples severe and sharp-tongued they can hardly be blamed if they sigh and turn away from Him.

All this is more than a theory. Unholy tempers

OF GOD AND MEN

among professed saints constitute a plague and a pestilence. The low state of religion in our day is largely due to the lack of public confidence in religious people.

It is time we Christians stop trying to excuse our un-Christlike dispositions and frankly admit our failure to live as we should. Wesley said that we will not injure the cause of Christ by admitting our sins, but that we are sure to do so by denying them.

There is a remedy for inward evil. There is a power in Christ that can enable the worst of us to live lives of purity and love. We have but to seek it and to lay hold of it in faith. God will not disappoint us.

Books and Moral Standards

THE LATE JIMMY WALKER, playboy mayor of New York during the roaring twenties, once delivered himself of a quip that was widely quoted as being the distilled essence of something or other and was unfortunately accepted as gospel truth by those who wanted to believe it. "I have never heard," said Jimmy, "of anyone who was ruined by a book."

These profound words were tossed off, as near as I can at the moment remember, during an official inquiry into the effect of certain questionable literature upon the morals of the reading public.

Now I can offer no proof that Mr. Walker had ever heard of anyone who had been ruined by a book, but that could only mean that the gentleman's knowledge on the subject was vastly small or that his idea of what it means to be "ruined" was not the same as that of the more conscientious persons within our population who still feel bothered about the effect of bad reading upon the collective public mind. Whatever the explanation, Mr. Walker's implication that no one had ever been ruined by a bad book is 100 per cent false. The facts are against it.

History will show that bad books have ruined not only individuals but whole nations as well. What the writings of Voltaire and Rousseau did to France is too well known to need further mention here. Again, it would not be difficult to establish a cause and effect relationship between the philosophy of Friedrich Nietzsche and the bloody career of Adolph Hitler. Certainly the doctrines of Nietzsche appeared again in the mouthings of der Fuhrer and soon became the official party line for the Nazi propagandists. And it is hardly conceivable that Russian Communism could have come into being apart from the writings of Karl Marx.

The truth is that thoughts are things and words are seeds. The printed word may lie unnoticed like a seed through the long winter, only to burst out when a favorable time comes and produce an abundant crop in belief and practice. Many who are today useful members of the church were brought to Christ by the reading of a book. Thousands have witnessed to the power of the lowly gospel tract to capture the mind and focus the attention on God and salvation.

Just what part evil literatre has played in the present moral breakdown throughout the world will never be known till men are called forth to answer to a holy God for their unholy deeds, but it must be very great indeed. For thousands of young people the first doubt about God and the Bible came with the reading of some evil book. We must respect the power of ideas. And printed ideas are as powerful as spoken ones; they may have a longer fuse but their explosive power is just as great.

What all this adds up to is that we Christians are bound in all conscience to discourage the reading of subversive literature and to promote as fully as possible the circulation of good books and magazines. Our Christian faith teaches us to expect to answer for every idle word; how much more severely shall we be held to account for every *evil* word, whether printed or spoken. We must see to it that we are never found on the side of a bad book nor on the other side from a good one.

Tolerance of noxious literature is not a mark of intellectual size; it may be a mark of a secret sympathy with evil. Every book should stand or fall on its merit, altogether apart from the reputation of its author. The fact that a nasty and suggestive book was written by an accepted writer does not make it the less harmful. Christians should judge a book by its purity, not by the reputation of its author.

The desire to appear broad-minded is one not easy to overcome, for it is rooted in our ego and is simply a none-too-subtle form of pride. In the name of broad-mindedness many a Christian home has been opened to literature that sprang not from a broad mind, but from a mind little and dirty and polluted with evil.

We require our children to wipe their feet before entering the house. Dare we demand less of the literature that comes into our home?

The Use and Abuse of Humor

FEW THINGS ARE as useful in the Christian life as a gentle sense of humor and few things are as deadly as a sense of humor out of control.

Many lose the race of life through frivolity. Paul is careful to warn us. He says plainly that the Christian's characteristic mood should not be one of jesting and foolish talking but rather one of thanksgiving (Eph. 5: 1-5). It is significant that in this passage the apostle classifies levity along with uncleanness, covetousness and idolatry.

Now obviously an appreciation of the humorous is not an evil in itself. When God made us He included a sense of humor as a built-in feature, and the normal human being will possess this gift in some degree at least. The source of humor is ability to perceive the incongruous. Things out of focus appear funny to us and may stir within us a feeling of amusement that will break into laughter.

Dictators and fanatics have no sense of humor. Hitler never knew how funny he looked, nor did Mussolini know how ridiculous he sounded as he solemnly mouthed his bombastic phrases. The religious fanatic will look upon situations so comical as to excite uncontrollable mirth in normal persons and see nothing amusing in them. This blind spot in his make-up prevents him from seeing how badly his own life and beliefs are out of focus. And just so far as he is blind to the incongruous he is abnormal; he is not quite as God meant him to be.

Humor is one thing, but frivolity is quite another. Cultivation of a spirit that can take nothing seriously is one of the great curses of society, and within the church it has worked to prevent much spiritual blessing that otherwise would have descended upon us. We have all met those people who will not be serious. They meet everything with a laugh and a funny remark. This is bad enough in the world, but positively intolerable among Christians.

Let us not allow a perverted sense of humor to ruin us. Some things are funny, and we may well laugh sometimes. But sin isn't funny; death isn't funny. There is nothing funny about a world tottering upon the brink of destruction; nothing funny about war and the sight of boys dying in blood upon the field of battle; nothing funny about the millions who perish each year without ever having heard the gospel of love.

It is time that we draw a line between the false and the true, between the things that are incidental and the things that are vital. Lots of things we can afford to let pass with a smile. But when humor takes religion as the object of its fun it is no longer natural—it is sinful and should be denounced for what it is and avoided by everyone who desires to walk with God.

Innumerable lectures have been delivered, songs sung and books written exhorting us to meet life with a grin and to laugh so the world can laugh with us; but let us remember that however jolly we Christians may become, the devil is not fooling. He is cold-faced and serious, and we shall find at last that he was playing for keeps. If we who claim to be followers of the Lamb will not take things seriously, Satan will, and he is wise enough to use our levity to destroy us.

I am not arguing for unnatural solemnity; I see no value in gloom and no harm in a good laugh. My plea is for a great seriousness which will put us in mood with the Son of Man and with the prophets and apostles of the Scriptures. The joy of the

Lord can become the music of our hearts and the cheerfulness of the Holy Spirit will tune the harps within us. Then we may attain that moral happiness which is one of the marks of true spirituality, and also escape the evil effects of unseemly humor.

On Calling Our Brother a Fool

ONE OF THE hardest sayings in the New Testament is this: "Whosoever shall say to his brother, Raca, shall be in danger of the council: but whosoever shall say, Thou fool, shall be in danger of hell fire" (Matt. 5: 22).

What our Lord is saying here is not that a man will be punished with hell fire for calling another a fool, but that a man who can say "Thou fool" to a fellow man is revealing a state of heart which will fit him for hell in the end. Not the relatively slight offense of *calling* a brother a fool, but the serious sin of *feeling contempt* endangers a man's future. The gravity of the situation lies not in the fact that a man can cry "Fool!" but that he can entertain in his heart the contempt which the word expresses.

Contempt for a human being is an affront to God

almost as grave as idolatry, for while idolatry is disrespect for God Himself, contempt is disrespect for the being He made in His own image. Contempt says of a man, "Raca! This fellow is of no worth. I attach to his person no value whatsoever." The man guilty of thus appraising a human being is thoroughly bad.

Contempt is an emotion possible only where there is great pride. The error in moral judgment that undervalues another always springs out of the error that overvalues oneself. The contemptuous man esteems himself too highly, and for reasons that are invalid. His high opinion of himself is not based upon his position as a being made in God's image; he esteems himself for fancied virtues which he does not possess. He is wrong in his attitude toward himself and doubly wrong in his estimation of his fellow man. The error in his judgment is moral, not intellectual.

It is in the realm of religion that contempt finds its most fruitful soil and flourishes most luxuriantly. It is seen in the cold disdain with which the respectable church woman regards the worldly sister and in the scorn heaped upon the fallen woman by the legally married wife. The sober deacon may find it hard to conceal his contempt for the neighbor who drinks. The evangelical may castigate the liberal in a manner that leaves slight doubt that he feels himself above him in every way. Religion that is not purified by penitence, humility and love will lead to a feeling of contempt for the irreligious and the morally degraded. And since contempt implies a judgment of no worth made against a human brother, the contemptuous man comes under the displeasure of God and lies in danger of hell fire.

The Christian cannot close his eyes to good and evil in his fellow men. He cannot avoid rendering moral judgment on the deeds of men; and, indeed, he is accountable to do so. "By their fruits ye shall know them." "From such turn away." But his disapprobation of the evil ways of men must not betray him into contempt for them as human beings. He must reverence the humanity of every man, however degraded, out of appreciation for his divine origin. No one for whom Christ died can be common or worthless. Humanity itself must be honored as the garment assumed by the Eternal Son in the Incarnation. To esteem anyone worthless who wears the form of a man is to be guilty of an affront to the Son of Man. We should hate sin in ourselves and in all men, but we should never undervalue the man in whom the sin is found.

Magic No Part of the Christian Faith

ALL MAGIC PRACTICES are essentially alike in that they are based upon three erroneous assumptions.

These are: (1) That natural substances possess moral and spiritual qualities or that such qualities can be imparted to them. (2) That God is capricious and that His laws are whimsical and easily circumvented. (3) That there are invisible beings who can be persuaded to aid men or injure them if certain gestures are made or if certain secret words are mumbled, or if some object is worn, caressed or hung on the wall.

We are all acquainted with those milder manifestations of magic such as fear of beginning a journey on Friday, the bad luck that follows the breaking of a mirror or walking under a ladder. The good people of the Pennsylvania Dutch region where I grew up had their hexes, their tokens and their lucky charms, and believed in them implicitly. We younger ones tried to laugh off these things but I doubt whether any of us escaped the bondage entirely. To this day I feel for a moment a bit uneasy if I chance to glimpse the new moon over my left shoulder!

A belief in magic was thought by the late Sir James G. Frazer to be the only truly universal faith, being accepted as it is in some form by all the peoples of the world without exception. Against belief in the power of magic Moses and the prophets of Israel aimed some of their most devastating attacks. Yet when Christ came to Israel He found the people in bondage, not to the Law of Moses as some have supposed, but to the fear that grew out of the superstitious notions introduced into the pure religion of the Old Testament.

God had, for instance, commanded the Jews to wear upon their persons selected passages of Scripture to remind them of their responsibility to obey the Word and love the Lord supremely. By the time of Christ this practice had degenerated into pure superstition. The phylactery had taken on magical qualities. The Sabbath which God had given to be man's servant had become his master. The simple custom of washing the hands before eating had become a sacred ritual and its observance or nonobservance a test of godliness.

The temptation to attribute supernatural powers, or at least moral qualities, to inanimate objects is one almost impossible to resist. It is as if the human mind *wanted* to have it so, and I am not sure but it does. Sin has done strange things to us.

True Christian experience is direct knowledge of God. It is intimate fellowship between two personalities, God and the individual worshiper. The grounds of fellowship are mental, moral and spiritual, and these are precisely what material objects do not and cannot possess. The union of the human soul with God in Christ establishes a personal relationship which cannot be in any way affected by material substances.

The only spiritual qualities material things can possess are those we first gratuitously assign to them. We may agree, for instance, that a wedding ring shall stand for faithfulness in marriage, but the ring in itself is merely a piece of metal; it has no intrinsic meaning of any kind. The same bit of gold that tells a bride that her groom will be true to her could just as well crown a tooth or serve as a point for a fountain pen.

Christianity is basically a religion of meanings, and meaning belongs to intelligent beings only. The church by pronouncing certain objects sacred and attributing power to them has turned from the pure freedom of the gospel to a kind of educated magic, not as base perhaps as a hex or a chain letter, but far from New Testament truth nevertheless, and gravely injurious to the souls of man.

So strong is the bent of the human heart toward magic that there has hardly been a time when the faith of Christ has not been plagued with it. Our Lord swept aside material objects as having no spiritual significance and placed the worship of God in the spirit, where it properly belongs. He also warned against the belief that words even when spoken in prayer have any essential value other than that imparted to them by the worshiper. Prayer that takes its value from the number of times certain words are repeated is pagan, not Christian. "But when ye pray, use not vain repetitions, as the heathen do: for they think that they shall be heard for their much speaking" (Matt. 6: 7).

The apostles also labored hard to free the young church from the power of magic, that is, from belief in the spiritual significance of material objects. Circumcision, new moons, foods, they said, had no power to make a man either good or bad. Words, Paul insisted, had no value as mere religious sounds. They must express meanings or they could have no significance for speaker or hearer. This idea Paul developed fully in the fourteenth chapter of his first Corinthian epistle. It is too bad we cannot remember it.

Our Heavenly Father gave us the beautiful, diversified creation as a kind of birthday present; all is to be received thankfully and nothing is to be despised. But always we must keep in mind that it is living personality that gives meaning to the world. Material objects neither hate nor love; they are neither good nor evil. We need not fear them and we should not attribute to them qualities they do not possess.

Our responsibility is to God and our fellowship is with Him. With magic or superstition in any form the Christian should simply have nothing to do.

No Christian Should Feel Resentment

I HAVE BEEN around religious circles quite a long time and I have never heard the word *resent* used by a victorious man. Or at least if he used the word it was not to express any feelings within his own heart.

In the course of scores of conferences and hundreds of conversations I have many times heard people say, "I resent that." But I repeat: I have never heard the words used by a victorious man. Resentment simply cannot dwell in a loving heart. Before resentfulness can enter, love must take its flight and bitterness take over. The bitter soul will compile a list of slights at which it takes offense and will watch over itself like a mother bear over her cubs. And the figure is apt, for the resentful heart is always surly and suspicious like a she-bear.

Few sights are more depressing than that of a professed Christian defending his supposed rights and bitterly resisting any attempt to violate them. Such a Christian has never accepted the way of the cross. The sweet graces of meekness and humility are unknown to him. He grows every day harder and more acrimonious as he defends his reputation, his rights, his ministry, against his imagined foes.

The only cure for this sort of thing is to die to self and rise with Christ into newness of life. The man who sets the will of God as his goal will reach that goal, not by self-defense but by self-abnegation. Then no matter what sort of treatment he receives from his fellow men he will be altogether at peace. The will of God has been done—whether by curses or compliments he cares not, for he seeks not one or the other but only to do the will of God at any cost. Then, whether riding the crest of public favor or dwelling in the shadow of obscurity, he will be content. If there be some who take pleasure in holding him down, still he will not resent them, for he seeks not advancement but the will of God.

It is sad that certain pagan philosophers have had to teach us Christians so simple a lesson as this. "I must die," said Epictetus, "and must I die groaning too? I must be exiled; and what hinders me, then, but that I may go smiling, and cheerful, and serene? 'Betray a secret.' I will not betray it. 'Then I will fetter you.' You will fetter my leg, but no one can get the better of my free will. 'I will behead that paltry body of yours.' Did I ever tell you," answered Epictetus, "that I alone had a head that couldn't be cut off?

"This it is to have studied what ought to be studied; to have placed our desires and aversions above tyranny and above chance. I must die—if instantly, I will die instantly; if in a short time, I will dine first, and when the hour comes, then will I die. How? As becomes one who restores what is not his own."

Let no one reject the reasoning of this sturdy old philosopher. Without the light of saving grace he yet knew how a created being ought to behave beneath the mighty hand of his Creator, and that is more than many Christians appear to know.

But we have better authority than his for our conduct. Christ left us an example, and from it there can be no appeal. As He was so are we in this world, and He felt no trace of resentment against any man. Even those who crucified Him were forgiven while they were in the act. Not a word did He utter against them nor against the ones who stirred them up to destroy Him. How evil they all were He knew better than any other man, but He maintained toward them an attitude of charitable understanding. They were only doing their duty, and even those who ordered them to their grisly task were unaware of the meaning of their act. To Pilate He said, "Thou couldest have no power at all against me, except it were given thee from above." So He referred everything back to the will of God and rose above the swampland of personalities. He held no grudge against any man. He felt no resentment.

The worst feature about this whole thing is that it does no good to call attention to it. The bitter heart is not likely to recognize its own condition, and if the resentful man reads this he will smile smugly and think I mean someone else. In the meantime he will grow smaller and smaller trying to get bigger, and he will become more and more obscure trying to become known. As he pushes on toward his selfish goal his very prayers will be surly accusations against the Almighty and his whole relationship toward other Christians will be one of suspicion and distrust.

As Spurgeon said of someone, May the grass grow green on his grave when he dies, for nothing ever grew around him while he lived.

Beware the Vexed Spirit

SOME TIME AGO I heard a prayer uttered by a servant of God who was deeply grieved over the lack of spirituality in the church of which he was the pastor. His prayer was, "O Lord, let me not become vexed with the ways of my people."

Always it is more important that we retain a right spirit toward others than that we bring them to our way of thinking, even if our way is right.

Satan has achieved a real victory when he succeeds in getting us to react in an unspiritual way toward sins and failures in our brethren. We cannot fight sin with sin or draw men to God by frowning at them in fleshly anger. "For the wrath of man worketh not the righteousness of God."

Often acts done in a spirit of religious irrritation have consequences far beyond anything we could have guessed. Moses allowed himself to become vexed with Israel and in a fit of pique smote the rock. With the same stroke he closed the land of promise against him for the rest of his life.

It is a splendid rule to refrain from making decisions when we are discouraged. Elijah, in an attack of self-pity, prayed that his life might be taken —and his active ministry ended right there. After that he did no more than get ready for his departure. God raised up another man to carry on and took his dissatisfied servant away. Piqued prayers can be dangerous.

I heard of a certain man of God who had been greatly used in praying for the sick with the natural result that he was often called out at very inopportune times and under circumstances that were anything but pleasant. Once when sent for in the middle of the night he threw himself across the bed and complained to God of the lack of consideration the call evinced. That was the end for him. Thereafter no one was ever delivered in answer to his prayer, even though he sought with many tears to capture again the gift he had lost.

It is quite natural, and even spiritual, to feel sorrow and heaviness when we see the professed followers of Christ walking in the ways of the world. And our first impulse may easily be to go straight to them and upbraid them indignantly. But such methods are seldom successful. The heat in our spirit may not be from the Holy Ghost, and if it is not then it can very well do more harm than good.

It is not an easy task to be prophets and reformers in our generation and yet maintain a spirit of kindliness toward the very ones we are sent to reprove. But it is not impossible. "It is God which worketh in you both to will and to do of his good pleasure." He can do the impossible if we but yield and obey. He will meet our faith with a calm, deep fire of holy hatred for sin expressed in a manner consistent with love.

In this as in everything else Christ is our perfect example. A prayerful, face-down meditation on the life of Christ will show us how to oppose with kindness and reprove with charity. And the power of the Holy Spirit within us will enable us to follow His blessed example.

On Backing Into Our Convictions

TOO MANY OF our religious convictions are negative. We act not from a positive conviction that something is right, but from a feeling that the opposite is wrong.

We become allergic to certain beliefs and practices and react violently from them. Thus our re-actions become actions; we are driven to our posi-tions by the enemy rather than led to them by the truth.

The bad reasoning back of this kind of thing is the assumption that if a man is wrong on one thing he is wrong on everything, so that if a liberal or a cultist is known to favor a belief we shy away from the belief, not because we know why it is wrong but because we know who holds it. We are thus always on the defensive; we back into our positions like stubborn horses rather than walk into them face forward like obedient sheep. The way to be right, so we reason, is to watch the enemy, discover what he favors, and then choose the opposite.

That many of our hotly defended beliefs are no more than reactions from what we consider false doctrine it would not be difficult to prove. The doc-trine of justification by works, for instance, itself a serious error, has driven some teachers to espouse the equally damaging error of salvation without a good life. To many persons the very thought of "works" is repugnant because of its association with the effete Judaism of New Testament times and the Romanism of more recent days. The upshot of the matter is that we have salvation without righteous-ness and right doctrine without right deeds. Grace is twisted out of its moral context and made the cause of lowered standards of conduct in the church.

Again, the fear of legalism has driven some of God's good people to positions so grotesque as to be ridiculous. Some years ago in a religious paper I came across an example of this kind of negative doctrine. In order to make clear the difference between law and grace, a writer argued that if a murderer came to him and inquired how to be saved he would not dare say, "Turn away from your old life, cease to commit murder and believe on Jesus Christ." That, said the writer, would be mixing law and grace. All he could say to be scriptural, he reasoned, would be "Believe on the Lord Jesus Christ and thou shalt be saved." Such unholy teaching could not possibly come from the Scriptures; it could only result from the writer's frightened retreat from the error of salvation by works.

We have noticed very much the same thing in our standard attitude toward science, evolution and various philosophies which we believe to be contrary to or unsympathetic with the Christian faith. Our reaction to these enemies is one of wild flight. We use up a lot of ammunition, but we waste it in a rearguard action that can at best only slow up what is too patently a retreat.

Now the truth is that Christianity can stand on its own legs. Christ does not need our nervous defense. The church must not allow herself to be maneuvered into fighting her enemy's war, letting the unbelieving world decide what she is to believe and where and when she is to act. As long as she does this she is falling short of her privileges in Christ Jesus.

"Ye shall receive power," said our Lord to His

disciples, and "power" means "ability to do." It is God's purpose to give us ample power to carry the fight to the enemy instead of sitting passively by and allowing the enemy to carry the fight to us. If anyone is to go on the defensive it should never be the church. The truth is self-validating and self-renewing; its whole psychology is that of attack. Its own vigorous attack is all the defense it needs.

Could it be that the deep cause behind all this frightened defensive action on the part of the evangelicals today is the failure of so many leaders to have a true spiritual experience of their own? It is hard to see how any man who has seen heaven opened and has heard the voice of God speaking to his own heart can ever be uncertain about the truth he is to hold or the message he must proclaim.

We Can be Delivered From Carnal Fear

CARNAL FEAR MAY take either of two opposite directions. It may make us afraid to do what we know we should do, or afraid not to do what we have reason to think people expect us to do.

97

There is a foolish consistency which brings us into bondage to the consciences of other people. Our Christian testimony has created a certain expectation in the minds of our friends, and rather than jeopardize our standing with them we dutifully act in accordance with their expectations even though we have no personal conviction about the matter. We are simply afraid not to do what people expect of us. We cannot face our public after we have failed to do what we know they expected us to do.

This morality by public pressure is not pure morality at all. At best it is a timid righteousness of doubtful parentage; at worst it is the child of weakness and fear. A free Christian should act from within with a total disregard for the opinions of others. If a course is right he should take it because it is right, not because he is afraid not to take it. And if it is wrong he should avoid it though he lose every earthly treasure and even his very life as a consequence.

Fear of the opinion of the group tends to regiment the members of denominations and churches and force them into a cooky-cutter uniformity. The desire to stand well within our own circle of religious friends destroys originality and makes imitators of us. Various churches have their approved experiences, their religious accents, even their accepted religious tones; these become standard for the group and are to the local fellowship what circumcision was to Israel, a ceremonial token of acceptance into the clan.

The great fault in all this is that it shifts the life motivation from within to without, from God to our fellow man. Any act done because we are afraid not to do it is of the same moral quality as the act that is not done because we are afraid to do it. Fear, not love and faith, dictates the conduct, and whatsoever is not of faith is sin.

The way to escape this double snare is simple. Make a complete surrender to God; love Him with all your heart and love every man for His sake. Determine to obey your own convictions as they crystallize within you as a result of unceasing prayer and constant study of the Scriptures. After that you may safely ignore the expectations of your friends as well as the criticisms of your enemies. You will experience first the shocked surprise of the regimented army of lock-step believers, then their grudging admiration; and if you continue to walk the way of love and courage they may take heart from your example, throw off the bondage of fear and go forth as ransomed men and women to walk in the sweet liberty wherewith Christ has made them free.

Learning to Live with Our Problems

As we walk the Christian way we are likely to run into three different kinds of problems: (1) Problems which, if we just ignore them, will go away of themselves; (2) problems which we may pray our way out of, and (3) problems that will not go away and, for the time being, will not yield to the most importunate prayer.

It is the latter kind that we have in mind now.

We are all idealists. We picture to ourselves a life on earth completely free from every hindrance, a kind of spiritual Utopia where we can always control events, where we can move about as favorites of heaven, adjusting circumstances to suit ourselves. This we feel would be quite compatible with the life of faith and in keeping with the privileged place we hold as children of God.

In thinking thus we simply misplace ourselves; we mistake earth for heaven and expect conditions here below which can never be realized till we reach the better world above. While we live we may expect troubles, and plenty of them. We are never promised a life without problems as long as we remain among fallen men.

There is a sense in which God makes no difference between the saint and the sinner. He maketh His sun to rise on the evil and on the good, and sendeth rain on the just and on the unjust. It is strange that we rarely notice the other side of this truth: that God also visits His children with the usual problems common to all the sons of men. The Christian will feel the heat on a sweltering day; the cold will bite into his skin as certainly as into that of his unsaved neighbor; he will be affected by war and peace, booms and depressions, without regard to his spiritual state. To believe otherwise is to go beyond the Scriptures and to falsify the experience of the saints in every age.

What then are we to do about our problems? We must learn to live with them until such time as God delivers us from them. If we cannot remove them, then we must pray for grace to endure them without murmuring. Problems patiently endured will work for our spiritual perfecting. They harm us only when we resist them or endure them unwillingly.

Our Lord was surrounded with enemies from the moment of His birth. They constituted a real and lasting problem which He simply had to endure for the period of His earthly life. He escaped it only by dying.

Paul had his thorn in the flesh. We do not know for sure what it was, but it required large supplies of grace to enable him to endure it. At first he thought it belonged among the things he could pray his way out of, but at last he was compelled to learn to live with it. The forceful masculine Paul must have been humbled by this experience. His whole temperament would lead him to attack this thing in bold, determined prayer, to rush upon it like David and drive it from him for good. And that would have been a thrilling thing to do. It was less colorful to admit temporary defeat and adjust himself to the presence of an unsolved problem; but by so doing he gained a lesson he could have learned no other way. Paul was a better man for his thorn.

The pastor may expect to meet with real obstacles while he shepherds his flock; the Christian business-man will have his troubles; the students, the house-wife, the professional man, the laborer, the states-man, will all feel the abrasive action of long-enduring unsolved problems.

We should both hope and quietly wait for the sal-vation of God. And "if thou faint in the day of adversity, thy strength is small."

Let's Cultivate Simplicity and Solitude

WE CHRISTIANS MUST simplify our lives or lose untold treasures on earth and in eternity.

Modern civilization is so complex as to make the devotional life all but impossible. It wears us out by multiplying distractions and beats us down by destroying our solitude, where otherwise we might drink and renew our strength before going out to face the world again.

"The thoughtful soul to solitude retires," said the poet of other and quieter times; but where is the solitude to which we can retire today? Science, which has provided men with certain material comforts, has robbed them of their souls by surrounding them with a world hostile to their existence. "Commune with your own heart upon your bed and be still" is a wise and healing counsel, but how can it be followed in this day of the newspaper, the telephone, the radio and the television? These modern playthings, like pet tiger cubs, have grown so large and dangerous that they threaten to devour us all. What was intended to be a blessing has become a positive curse. No spot is now safe from the world's intrusion.

One way the civilized world destroys men is by

preventing them from thinking their own thoughts.

Our "vastly improved methods of communication" of which the shortsighted boast so loudly now enable a few men in strategic centers to feed into millions of minds alien thought stuff, ready-made and pre-digested. A little effortless assimilation of these borrowed ideas and the average man has done all the thinking he will or can do. This subtle brainwashing goes on day after day and year after year to the eternal injury of the populace—a populace, incidentally, which is willing to pay big money to have the job done, the reason being, I suppose, that it relieves them of the arduous and often frightening task of reaching independent decisions for which they must take responsibility.

There was a time, not too long ago, when a man's home was his castle, a sure retreat to which he might return for quietness and solitude. There "the rains of heaven may blow in, but the king himself cannot enter without permission," said the proud British, and made good on their boast. That was home indeed. It was of such a sacred place the poet sang:

> O, when I am safe in my sylvan home,
> I tread on the pride of Greece and Rome;
> And when I am stretched beneath the pines,
> Where the evening star so holy shines,
> I laugh at the lore and the pride of man,
> At the sophist schools, and the learned clan;
> For what are they all, in their high conceit,
> When man in the bush with God may meet?*

---

* *Good-bye*, Ralph Waldo Emerson.

While it is scarcely within the scope of the present piece, I cannot refrain from remarking that the most ominous sign of the coming destruction of our country is the passing of the American home. Americans live no longer in homes, but in theaters. The members of many families hardly know each other, and the face of some popular TV star is to many wives as familiar as that of their husbands. Let no one smile. Rather should we weep at the portent. It will do no good to wrap ourselves in the Stars and Stripes for protection. No nation can long endure whose people have sold themselves for bread and circuses. Our fathers sleep soundly, and the harsh bedlam of commercialized noise that engulfs us like something from Dante's Inferno cannot disturb their slumber. They left us a goodly heritage. To preserve that heritage we must have a national character as strong as theirs. And this can be developed only in the Christian home.

The need for solitude and quietness was never greater than it is today. What the world will do about it is their problem. Apparently the masses want it the way it is and the majority of Christians are so completely conformed to this present age that they, too, want things the way they are. They may be annoyed a bit by the clamor and by the goldfish bowl existence they live, but apparently they are not annoyed enough to do anything about it. However, there are a few of God's children who have had enough. They want to relearn the ways of solitude and simplicity and gain the infinite riches of the interior life. They want to discover the blessed-

ness of what Dr. Max Reich called "spiritual alone-
ness." To such I offer a brief paragraph of counsel.

Retire from the world each day to some private
spot, even if it be only the bedroom (for a while I
retreated to the furnace room for want of a better
place). Stay in the secret place till the surrounding
noises begin to fade out of your heart and a sense of
God's presence envelops you. Deliberately tune out
the unpleasant sounds and come out of your closet
determined not to hear them. Listen for the inward
Voice till you learn to recognize it. Stop trying to
compete with others. Give yourself to God and then
be what and who you are without regard to what
others think. Reduce your interests to a few. Don't
try to know what will be of no service to you. Avoid
the digest type of mind—short bits of unrelated facts,
cute stories and bright sayings. Learn to pray inwardly every moment. After a while you can do
this even while you work. Practice candor, childlike
honesty, humility. Pray for a single eye. Read less,
but read more of what is important to your inner
life. Never let your mind remain scattered for very
long. Call home your roving thoughts. Gaze on
Christ with the eyes of your soul. Practice spiritual
concentration.

All the above is contingent upon a right relation
to God through Christ and daily meditation on the
Scriptures. Lacking these, nothing will help us;
granted these, the discipline recommended will go
far to neutralize the evil effects of externalism and
to make us acquainted with God and our own souls.

The Christian Is the True Realist

SOME SHALLOW THINKERS dismiss the Christian as an unrealistic person who lives in a make-believe world. "Religion," they say, "is a flight from reality. To embrace it is to take refuge in dreams."

By constantly arguing thus they have managed to disturb a great many persons and to create in many minds a gnawing doubt concerning the soundness of the Christian position. But there is nothing to be disturbed about. A better acquaintance with the facts will dispel all doubts and convince the believer that his expectations are valid and his faith well grounded.

If realism is the recognition of things as they actually are, the Christian is of all persons the most realistic. He of all intelligent thinkers is the one most concerned with reality. He insists that his beliefs correspond with facts. He pares things down to their stark essentials and squeezes out of his mind everything that inflates his thinking. He demands to know the whole truth about God, sin, life, death, moral accountability and the world to come. He wants to know the worst about himself in order that he may do something about it. Something in him refuses to be cheated, however pleasant the deception might be to his self-esteem. He takes into account the undeniable fact that he has sinned. He recognizes the shortness of time and the certainty of death. These he does not try to avoid or alter to his own liking. They are facts and he faces them full on. He is a realist.

We of the Christian faith need not go onto the defensive. The man of the world is the dreamer, not the Christian. The sinner can never be quite himself. All his life he must pretend. He must act as if he were never going to die, and yet he knows too well that he is. He must act as if he had not sinned, when in his deep heart he knows very well that he has. He must act unconcerned about God and judgment and the future life, and all the time his heart is deeply disturbed about his precarious condition. He must keep up a front of nonchalance while shrinking from facts and wincing under the lash of conscience. The news of a friend's sudden death leaves him shaken with the suggestion that he may be next, but he dare not show this; he must cover his terror the best he can and continue to act his part. All his adult life he must dodge and hide and conceal. When he finally drops the act he either loses his mind or tries suicide.

> "Say, poor worldling, can it be
> That my heart should envy thee?"

On to El-beth-el!

JACOB, AFTER HIS memorable experience in the wilderness, where he saw a ladder set up on the earth and saw God standing above it, called the place of his encounter Beth-el, which means "the house of God," *beth* being house and *el*, God.

Many years later, after he had suffered and sinned and repented and discovered the worthlessness of all earthly things, had been conquered and blessed by God at Peniel and had seen the face of God in an hour of spiritual agony, he renamed the place *El-beth-el*, which means "the God of the house of God." Historically the place was always known as Beth-el, but in Jacob's worshiping heart it would forever be El-beth-el.

The change is significant. Jacob had shifted his emphasis from the house to the One whom he met there. God Himself now took the center of his interest. He had at last been converted from a place to God Himself. A blessed conversion.

Many Christians never get beyond Beth-el. God is in their thoughts, but He is not first. His name is spoken only after a hyphen has separated the primary interest from the secondary, God being secondary, the "house" first. The weakness of the denominational psychology is that it puts something else before God. Certainly there may be no intention to do so; the very thought may startle the innocent denominationalist; but where the emphasis is, there the heart is also. Loyalty to our group may be a fine thing, but when it puts God on the other side of a hyphen it is a bad thing. Always God must be first.

Faithfulness to the local church is also a good thing. The true Christian will, by a kind of spiritual instinct, find a body of believers somewhere, identify himself with it and try by every proper means to promote its growth and prosperity. And that, we repeat, is good. But when the church becomes so large and important that it hides God from our eyes it is no longer for us a good thing. Or better say that it is a good thing wrongly used. For the church was never intended to substitute for God. Let us understand that every local church embraces *El-beth-el* and the right balance will be found and maintained: God first and His house second.

I sometimes fear that theology itself may exist as a semiopaque veil behind which God, if seen at all, is seen only imperfectly. Theology is precious because it is the study of God. And the very English word in its composition puts God where He belongs —first. But God is often anything but first in much that is called theology. Too frequently He "standeth behind our wall, he looketh forth at the windows, shewing himself through the lattice." We talk endlessly about Him and fail completely to notice Him as He tries to attract our attention in actual experience.

Every means of grace is but a "house," a "place," and God must be there to make it significant. Any means that can be disassociated from God can be a snare if we do not watch it. It has not done anything for us till it has led us to God and put an *El* after it. But still it is incomplete, and will be until the *El* is placed *before* it. No soul has found its real place till all its places have God before them: God first—God on the near side of the hyphen.

We may judge our spiritual growth pretty accurately by observing the total emphasis of our heart. Where is the primary interest? Is it Beth-el or El-beth-el? Is it my church or my Lord? Is it my ministry or my God? My creed or my Christ? We are spiritual or carnal just as we are concerned with the house or with the God of the house. If we discover that religious things are first, separated from God by a hyphen, we should immediately go down in tender penitence before our Lord and pray that He will forgive us for this affront and correct our evil attitude. He will hear and, if we continue to seek Him in sincerity of heart, He will take His place in the center of our lives where He by every right belongs.

When we have gone on from Beth-el to El-beth-el the Triune God will become to us our home, our environment, our rest and our life. Then we shall know the deep, inner meaning of the Christian faith; but not till then.

Through God to Nature

THE CONCEPT OF nature held by modern men was, as far as I can see, completely unknown to the men who wrote the Bible.

To them nature meant an order or kind of life and the characteristics belonging to it. They spoke of "the nature of angels," "the divine nature" and being "Jews by nature," but the expression "the beauties of nature," in the sense we use it now, they simply would not have understood.

Modern science takes for its province all nature, which it conceives to be all existing things on earth and in the astronomical heavens. These it studies, searches into and classifies, and by generalizing from particular observations it comes up with natural "laws," another name for the way things behave and may be trusted to behave for the future.

One man studies the phenomena that lie around him to learn their secrets, to discover how things *are* and how they *work*. He is said to be engaging in "pure" science; that is, he is seeking knowledge for its own sake. As far as he is able to maintain his attitude of scientific detachment he gives no thought to any use his discoveries may be put to later on.

Another man takes the findings of pure science and makes them work to heal his friends, to destroy his enemies, to take the drudgery out of his life, to get him swiftly from one place to another. This man is engaging in "applied" science, which is, of course, only knowledge harnessed to a purpose, good or bad.

To a believer the ominous thing about all this is that God is not necessary to it. The man of science takes facts where he finds them. How things got here is of no interest to him as a scientist. The moment he allows any religious belief to influence his thinking he is a scientist no longer but in some measure a theologian and philosopher.

The same man may be both a scientist and a Christian, but there is no necessary relation between the two. There is no such thing as "Christian" science, just as there is no Christian chemistry or Christian mathematics. The modern vogue of bringing science to the support of Christianity proves not the truth of the Christian faith but the gnawing uncertainty in the hearts of those who must look to science to give respectability to their belief.

Art and literature are also concerned with nature. The poet never tires of rivers and seas, birds and flowers, sunshine and starlight and all the beautiful objects among which we all walk from birth to death, mostly without noticing them. His attitude toward nature is superior to that of the scientist, for it denotes admiration rather than mere curiosity or a selfish desire to make things work for him.

Every now and again someone comes out with a book purporting to show how it is possible to reach God through nature, but this stands in blunt contradiction to the teachings of the Bible. The first man to try to reach God through nature was Cain, and he failed. Nature cannot lift men to God nor serve as a ladder by which he may climb into the divine bosom.

The heavens and the earth were intended to be a semitransparent veil through which moral intelligences might see the glory of God (Psa. 19: 1-6; Rom. 1: 19, 20), but for sin-blinded men this veil has become opaque. They see the creation but do not see through it to the Creator; or what glimpses they do have are dim and out of focus. It is possible to spend a lifetime admiring God's handiwork without acknowledging the presence of the God whose handiwork it is.

So deep is my debt to the great poets of nature, particularly William Wordsworth, that it would be an act of base ingratitude to utter any word that might reflect upon them; but no true Christian can read them without a feeling of disappointment. True, they speak of God, but only at second hand. Theirs is not the God of the Bible, not the God revealed in Jesus Christ, but a vague and shadowy being almost indistinguishable from the forces of nature. Here is a fair sample from Wordsworth's "Prelude":

> *Wisdom and Spirit of the universe!*
> *Thou Soul that art the eternity of thought*

That givest to forms and images a breath
And everlasting motion . . .

With what joy the Christian turns from even the purest nature poets to the prophets and psalmists of the Scriptures. These saw God first; they rose by the power of faith to the throne of the Majesty on high and observed the created world from above. Their love of natural objects was deep and intense, but they loved them not for their own sakes but for the sake of Him who created them. They walked through the world as through the garden of God. Everything reminded them of Him. They saw His power in the stormy wind and tempest; they heard His voice in the thunder; the mountains told them of His strength and the rocks reminded them that He was their hiding place. The sun by day and the moon and stars by night spoke in the ear of reason and recited the story of their divine birth.

The nature poets are enamored of natural objects; the inspired writers are God-enamored men. That is the difference, and it is a vitally important one.

The Bible World Is the Real World

WHEN READING THE Scriptures the sensitive person is sure to feel the marked difference between the world as the Bible reveals it and the world as conceived by religious people today. And the contrast is not in our favor.

The world as the men and women of the Bible saw it was a personal world, warm, intimate, populated. Their world contained first of all the God who had created it, who still dwelt in it as in a sanctuary and who might be discovered walking among the trees of the garden if the human heart were but pure enough to feel and human eyes clear enough to see. And there were also also present many beings sent of God to be ministers to them who were the heirs of salvation. They also recognized the presence of sinister forces which it was their duty to oppose and which they might easily conquer by an appeal to God in prayer.

Christians today think of the world in wholly different terms. Science, which has brought us many benefits, has with them also brought us a world wholly different from that which we see in the Scriptures. Today's world consists of wide and limitless spaces, having here and there at remote distances from each other blind and meaningless bodies controlled only by natural laws from which they can never escape. That world is cold and impersonal and completely without inhabitants except for man, the little shivering ephemeral being that clings to the soil while he rides "round in earth's diurnal course with rocks and stones and trees."

How glorious is the world as men of the Bible knew it! Jacob saw a ladder set up on the earth with God standing above it and the angels ascending and descending upon it. Abraham and Balaam and Manoah and how many others met the angels of God and conversed with them. Moses saw God in the bush; Isaiah saw Him high and lifted up and heard the antiphonal chant filling the temple.

Ezekiel saw a great cloud and fire unfolding itself, and out of the midst thereof came the likeness of four living creatures. Angels were present to tell of Jesus' coming birth and to celebrate that birth when it took place in Bethlehem; angels comforted our Lord when He prayed in Gethsemane; angels are mentioned in some of the inspired epistles, and the Book of the Revelation is bright with the presence of strange and beautiful creatures intent upon the affairs of earth and heaven.

Yes, the true world is a populated world. The blind eyes of modern Christians cannot see the invisible but that does not destroy the reality of the spiritual creation. Unbelief has taken from us the comfort of a personal world. We have accepted the empty and meaningless world of science as the true one, forgetting that science is valid only when dealing with material things and can know nothing about God and spiritual world.

We must have faith; and let us not apologize for it, for faith is an organ of knowledge and can tell us more about ultimate reality than all the findings of science. We are not opposed to science, but we recognize its proper limitations and refuse to stop where it is compelled to stop. The Bible tells of another world too fine for the instruments of scientific research to discover. By faith we engage that world and make it ours. It is accessible to us through the blood of the everlasting covenant. If we will believe we may even now enjoy the presence of God and the ministry of His heavenly messengers. Only unbelief can rob us of this royal privilege.

The God of Grace Is the God of Nature

A NEW RICH mine would be opened in our consciousness if we could learn to recognize God in nature as well as in grace. For the God of nature is also the God of grace.

It is characteristic of the unregenerate man that he can see God in nature, and of the immature Christian that he can see God only in grace. The instructed Christian, however, is able to recognize God in creation as well as in redemption.

Because sin has injured us so deeply, and because the whole transaction of repentance and deliverance from the gilt and power of iniquity makes such a mighty impression upon us emotionally, we naturally tend to appreciate the work of God in redemption more than in nature. But everything God does is praiseworthy and deserves our deepest admiration. Whether He is making or redeeming a world, He is perfect in all His doings and glorious in all His goings forth. Yet the long, long ages, however far they may carry us into the mysteries of God, will still find us singing the praises of the Lamb that was slain. For it is hardly conceivable that we sinners can ever forget the wormwood and the gall. We human sinners above other creatures have benefited by His grace, so it is altogether natural that we above all others should magnify the blood that bought us and the mercy that pardoned our sins.

Yet we glorify God's redeeming grace no less when we glorify His creating and sustaining power. Undoubtedly the foundation stone of all possible thinking concerning God is the simple text, "In the beginning God created." There began everything that is or will ever be. Had there been no creation there could have been no fall and no redemption. In the mind of God all things occurred at once; but in the sequence of time creation comes first. When Christ stepped down to take a body and redeem fallen man He stepped into the framework of an already existent nature. The very body that was broken and the blood that was spilled were part of creation, the product of the skilled fingers of God the Father Almighty, maker of heaven and earth.

"Nature is all fair and good in itself," said an old saint, "and Grace was sent out to save Nature and destroy sin, and bring again fair Nature to the blessed point from which it came: that is God. . . . Thus are Nature and Grace of one accord. . . . God is two in manner of working and one in love; and neither of these worketh without the other; they be not disparted."

If we miss seeing God in His works we deprive ourselves of the sight of a royal display of wisdom and power so elevating, so ennobling, so awe-inspiring as to make all attempts at description futile. Such a sight the angels behold day and night forever and ask nothing more to make them perpetually satisfied.

Let us learn to admire God in all things, great and small—in the soft play of a kitten on the rug as well as in the vast and breath-taking sweep of some galaxy around a point so remote as to stun the imagination and make language dumb. The first sight of God in salvation is as the dim early rays of a day a-borning, and the first feeble "Abba Father" of the new Christian is but the infant talk of a whole man yet to be.

Yes, there is more for us than we have yet known. If we will obey and believe we can go on pushing back the narrow borders of our spiritual world until it takes in the whole creation of God. And it is all ours, we are Christ's, and Christ is God's.

Two men stood on the shore watching the sun come up out of the sea. One was a merchant from London, the other was the poet, William Blake. As the bright yellow disk of the sun emerged into view, gilding the water and painting the sky with a thousand colors, the poet turned to the merchant and asked, "What do you see?" "Ah! I see gold," replied the merchant. "The sun looks like a great gold piece. What do you see?" "I see the glory of God," Blake answered, "and I hear a multitude of the heavenly host crying 'Holy, Holy, Holy is the Lord God Almighty. The whole earth is full of His glory.'"

God's Work Can Stand Inspection

WHEN GOD HAD created the heavens and the earth He looked them over and pronounced them very good. They stood inspection. Paul said of his religious activities, "This thing was not done in a corner." His ministry stood inspection.

The Lord through the ministry of Peter healed a man who had been lame from birth. The authorities later brought Peter before them and charged him with heresy, but their whole case collapsed because the healed man was there in plain sight. "And beholding the man which was healed standing with them, they could say nothing against it" (Acts 4: 14). Peter's ministry stood inspection.

We have never gone along with the tender-minded saints who fear to examine religious things lest God be displeased. On the contrary, we believe that God's handiwork is so perfect that it invites inspection. If God performs the work no matter how closely we look into it we may be sure that we will be forced to stand back in wonder and exclaim, "My Lord and my God." "I know that, whatsoever God doeth, it shall be for ever" (Eccl. 3: 14).

Of all work done under the sun religious work should be the most open to examination. There is positively no place in the church for sleight of hand or double talk. Everything done by the churches should be completely above suspicion. The true church will have nothing to hide. Her books will be available to anyone for inspection at any time. Her officers will insist upon an audit by someone from the outside.

A look at the habits of Ezra of the Old Testament and Paul of the New will show that these men would not allow themselves to be put in a position where an enemy might charge them with dishonesty. They insisted upon a fair count and a check by at least two responsible men to see that everything was done honestly and that no one could have reason to believe otherwise.

This principle of complete candor holds good also in the prayer life. When we are praying for something we have every right to look for the answer. Never should we fear to look at the facts. Either God answered or He did not, and there is no point in shutting our eyes and refusing to admit it when it is plain that no answer has been received. It may be that we shall need to trust Him without an answer and hold on quietly in prayer when our case looks hopeless. But we cannot help things by claiming He has answered when He has not.

A spirit of candor would do much to remove the widespread suspicion that Christian people are preoccupied with unrealities. Complete frankness with God, with our own souls and with our critics would take away many a sword from the hands of our enemies.

Many interpretations have been offered for our Lord's saying that we must become as little children to enter the kingdom of heaven. Just what quality does a child possess that Christians must have to please our Father who is in heaven? Could it be candor? The little child is so frank that he is often embarrassing to his elders. But maybe he has found the secret. It's well worth thinking about.

Praise in Three Dimensions

CHRIST IS TO HIS people so many wonderful things and brings to them such a wealth of benefits as the mind cannot comprehend nor the heart find words to express.

These treasures are both present and to come. The Spirit of Truth, speaking through Paul, assures us that God has in Christ blessed us with all spiritual blessings. These are ours as sons of the new creation and are made available to us now by the obedience of faith.

Peter, moved by the same Spirit, tells us of an inheritance guaranteed us by the resurrection of Christ, an inheritance incorruptible, undefiled and unfading, reserved in heaven for us.

There is no contradiction here, for one apostle speaks of present benefits and the other of benefits yet to be conferred upon us at the coming of Christ. And both exhaust human speech to celebrate the many blessings which we have already received.

Perhaps it would help us to understand if we thought of ourselves as fish in a vast river, at once enjoying the full flow of the stream, remembering with gratitude the current that has passed and awaiting with joyous anticipation the fullness that is moving on us from upstream. While this is but an imperfect figure of speech, it is quite literally true that we who trust in Christ are borne along by present grace while we remember with thankfulness the goodness we have enjoyed in days past and look forward in happy expectation to the grace and goodness that yet awaits us.

Bernard of Clairvaux speaks somewhere of a "perfume compounded of the remembered benefits of God." Such fragrance is too rare. Every follower of Christ should be redolent of such perfume; for have we not all received more from God's kindness than our imagination could have conceived before we knew Him and discovered for ourselves how rich and how generous He is?

That we have received of His fullness grace for grace no one will deny; but the fragrance comes not from the receiving; it comes from the remembering, which is something quite different indeed. Ten lepers received their health; that was the benefit. One came back to thank his benefactor; that was the perfume. Unremembered benefits, like dead flies, may cause the ointment to give forth a stinking savor.

Remembered blessings, thankfulness for present favors and praise for promised grace blend like myrrh and aloes and cassia to make a rare bouquet for the garments of the saints. With this perfume David also anointed his harp and the hymns of the ages have been sweet with it.

Perhaps it takes a purer faith to praise God for unrealized blessings than for those we once enjoyed or those we now enjoy. Yet many have risen to that sunlit peak, as did Anna Waring when she wrote,

> *Glory to Thee for all the grace*
> *I have not tasted yet . . .*

As we move into deeper personal acquaintance with the Triune God I think our life emphasis will shift from the past and the present to the future. Slowly we will become children of a living hope and sons of a sure tomorrow. Our hearts will be tender with memories of yesterday and our lives sweet with gratitude to God for the sure way we have come; but our eyes will be focused more and more upon the blessed hope of tomorrow.

Much of the Bible is devoted to prediction. Nothing God has yet done for us can compare with all that is written in the sure word of prophecy. And nothing He has done or may yet do for us can compare with *what He is and will be to us.* Perhaps the hymnist had this in mind when she sang,

> *"I have a heritage of joy*
> *That yet I must not see;*
> *The hand that bled to make it mine*
> *Is keeping it for me."*

Could that "heritage of joy" be less than the Beatific Vision?

The World to Come

IT HAS BEEN cited as a flaw in Christianity that it is more concerned with the world to come than with the world that now is, and some timid souls have been fluttering about trying to defend the faith of Christ against this accusation as a mother hen defends her chicks from the hawk.

Both the attack and the defense are wasted. No one who knows what the New Testament is about will worry over the charge that Christianity is otherworldly. Of course it is, and that is precisely where its power lies.

Christianity, which is faith in Christ, trust in His promises and obedience to His commandments, rests down squarely upon the Person of Christ. What He is, what He did and what He is doing—these provide a full guarantee that the Christian's hopes are valid. Christianity is what Christ says it is. His power becomes operative toward us as we accept His words as final and yield our souls to believe and obey.

Christ is not on trial; He needs no character witnesses to establish His trustworthiness. He came as the Eternal God in time's low tabernacle. He stands before no human tribunal, but all men stand before

Him now and shall stand for judgment at the last. Let any man bring the faith of Christ to the bar of man's opinion, let him try to prove that the teachings of Christ are in harmony with this philosophy or that religion and he is in fact rejecting Christ while seeking to defend Him. Ipse dixit, He has said it, is sufficient answer to all criticisms of Christ's claims.

Christianity has over the last half century been badly shaken by the criticisms of certain social philosophers. These gentlemen have assumed the basic soundness of the present world system. With a few improvements here and there a prosperous, healthy and peaceful society could be established right here on this earth, and to do this, say they, is the whole duty of man.

These men were observant enough to see that their concept of a permanently peaceful world was contrary to the teachings of the New Testament, so they quite naturally turned impatiently from them. Unfortunately many influential Christian leaders were not astute enough to notice the contradiction between the ipse dixits of Christ and the doctrines of the social dreamers and, smarting under the charges hurled at them by the one-world thinkers, they retreated from their Christian position and ran after the social philosophers crying "Me too, me too," in a frantic effort to prove that the world had misunderstood Christianity all along. In doing this they, of course, surrendered all that is unique in the faith of Christ and adopted an emaciated Christianity which is little more than a ghost of the faith once delivered.

Let no one apologize for the powerful emphasis Christianity lays upon the doctrine of the world to come. Right there lies its immense superiority to everything else within the whole sphere of human thought or experience. When Christ arose from death and ascended into heaven He established forever three important facts, namely, that this world has been condemned to ultimate dissolution, that the human spirit persists beyond the grave and that there is indeed a world to come.

There is about the Christian faith a quiet dogmatism, a cheerful intolerance. It feels no need to appease its enemies or compromise with its detractors. Christ came from God, out of eternity, to report on the things He had seen and heard and to establish true values for the confused human race. Then He drew a line between this world and the world to come and said in effect "Choose ye this day." The choice is between an earthly house which we can at best inhabit but a little while and the house of the Lord where we may dwell forevermore.

The Christian faith engages the profoundest problems the human mind can entertain and solves them completely and simply by pointing to the Lamb of God. The problems of origin and destiny have escaped the philosopher and the scientist, but the humblest follower of Christ knows the answer to both. "In the beginning" found Christ there at the creation of all things, and "the world to come" will find Him there at their regeneration.

The church is constantly being tempted to accept this world as her home, and sometimes she has listened to the blandishments of those who would woo her away and use her for their own ends. But if she is wise she will consider that she stands in the valley between the mountain peaks of eternity past and eternity to come. The past is gone forever and the present is passing as swift as the shadow on the sun dial of Ahaz. Even if the earth should continue a million years not one of us could stay to enjoy it. We do well to think of the long tomorrow.

Toward the world to come we are all headed. How unutterably wonderful that we Christians have one of our own kind to go ahead and prepare a place for us! That place will be in a world divinely ordered, beyond death and parting, where there is nothing that can hurt or make afraid.

> "Jerusalem the glorious!
>   The glory of the elect!
> O dear and future vision
>   That eager hearts expect!
> Even now by faith I see thee,
>   Even here thy walls discern;
> To thee my thoughts are kindled,
>   And strive, and pant, and yearn."

Maranatha! Glad Day!

WE MUST MEET the present emergency with a spirit of optimism. This is no time for repining, no time for looking backward, no time for self-pity or defeated complaining. We are on the winning side and we cannot lose. "Lo, I am with you" makes ultimate defeat impossible.

Surely the days are evil and the times are waxing late, but the true Christian is not caught unawares. He has been forewarned of just such times as these and has been expecting them. Present events only confirm the long-range wisdom of Jesus Christ and prove the authenticity of the prophetic Word. So the believer actually turns defeat into victory and draws strength from the knowledge that the Lord in whom he trusts has foretold events and is in full command of the situation.

Let us beware allowing our spiritual comforts to rise and fall with world news or the changing political and economic situation. We who lean upon Jesus and trust in the watchful love of a heavenly Father are not dependent upon those things for our peace.

It is not a pleasant thing to see a group of Christians huddled around the radio listening with worried faces to the newscaster or to the commentator painting lurid pictures of atomic bombs or the destruction of whole populations by bacteriological warfare. Where is our faith? Where is our confidence in the final triumph of Christ? All that these gentlemen say may be true. We have no desire to deny that the signs are ominous and the end is drawing near. But we refuse to get panicky, regardless.

It may easily be that before long one or another of our cities may go up in a puff of smoke and leave no one to tell how it happened. It may be that our own land may be invaded and made to suffer along with the other nations of the earth. We have been spared hitherto, but we have no guarantee for the future. God may yet chasten us with fire and blood for our presumptuous sins and for our highhanded flouting of His holy laws. No one can say for certain, but it could be.

But suppose it should be? Does that spell the defeat of all our hopes? Is our sense of security dependent upon the turn of events in Washington or Moscow? Is God the God of our better days and not the God of our sorrows too? Is there not a sure hope beyond the smoke and the rubble and the grave? Is there no difference between Egypt and the children of Israel? Is there not blood on a few doorposts here and there?

We must face today as children of tomorrow. We must meet the uncertainties of this world with the certainty of the world to come. To the pure in heart nothing really bad can happen. He may die, but what is death to a Christian? Not death but sin should be our great fear. Without doubt the heavens being on fire shall be dissolved, and the earth and the works that are therein shall be burned up. Sooner or later that will come. But what of it? Do not we, according to His promise, look for new heavens and a new earth, wherein dwelleth righteousness?

Surely this is not the time for pale faces and trembling knees among the sons of the new creation. The darker the night the brighter faith shines and the sooner comes the morning. Look up and lift up your heads; our redemption draweth near.